Self Awareness and Personal

Also by Chris Rose

THE PERSONAL DEVELOPMENT GROUP: The Student's Guide (2008)

Self Awareness and Personal Development

Resources for Psychotherapists and Counsellors

Edited by

Chris Rose

First published 2012 by
PALGRAVE MACMILLAN

Palgrave Macmillan in the UK is an imprint of Macmillan Publishers Limited, registered in England, company number 785998, of Houndmills, Basingstoke, Hampshire RG21 6XS.

Palgrave Macmillan in the US is a division of St Martin's Press LLC, 175 Fifth Avenue, New York, NY 10010.

Palgrave Macmillan is the global academic imprint of the above companies and has companies and representatives throughout the world.

Palgrave® and Macmillan® are registered trademarks in the United States, the United Kingdom, Europe and other countries.

ISBN: 978–0–230–24018–6

This book is printed on paper suitable for recycling and made from fully managed and sustained forest sources. Logging, pulping and manufacturing processes are expected to conform to the environmental regulations of the country of origin.

A catalogue record for this book is available from the British Library.

A catalog record for this book is available from the Library of Congress.

10 9 8 7 6 5 4 3 2 1
21 20 19 18 17 16 15 14 13 12

Printed and bound in Great Britain by
CPI Antony Rowe, Chippenham and Eastbourne

*To Amy, who one day might want to know
more about herself and others*

Contents

Acknowledgements

This book comes out of many experiences of trying to be aware of others and the accompanying realization that it is impossible without an awareness of self. Whether with clients, patients, trainees, supervisees, colleagues or with family and friends, these experiences have formed the foundation of this book, and I am grateful to all of them. However, the vignettes and case studies are (unless stated otherwise) fictitious creations based upon imagination and experience.

Particular thanks go to my fellow authors who have been an inspirational and co-operative team. Others have made valuable contributions behind the scenes: Hilary Prentice, Nick Totton, Zita Cox, Annie Browne, Stella McGuire and Peter Darch. Thanks also go to Catherine Gray at Palgrave Macmillan.

Preface

Although this book is not explicitly about groups, my own interest in group psychotherapy has informed much of the project. It is written by a group of authors, for example, with the idea that in learning from each other we can present a richer and more diverse account for the reader. Groups have many strengths. Not the least of these strengths is their capacity to demonstrate our mutual interdependence.

Therapy groups in particular are brilliant places to experience and learn about intersubjectivity. Every communication in whatever form triggers responses around the circle, and the struggle to both articulate and hear what is important reveals the complex web of communication that we are all part of. That is not to say that I have ever heard a group member say the word 'intersubjectivity'. Instead they might ask each other, 'So what's your end of the string?' Every word or gesture creates a reaction, and there is rich understanding to be found in the interplay. They have discovered that learning about both ends of the string can reveal new levels of insight and new ways of relating.

In many ways, this book is asking the same question. 'What's your end of the string?' It attempts to unravel some tangles and knots in order to become aware of the multiple dimensions of self and other. Above all it sets out to engage the reader's curiosity to expand their ideas and visions of themselves and others. As part of that process, it introduces the metaphor of the 'internal group', where the ways in which we communicate with ourselves can provide a rich resource for self understanding.

The metaphor is particularly useful for those working in individual therapy, because every encounter that goes beyond the superficial draws upon and engages multiple aspects of the self. In individual therapy there are always more than two people in the room. Experiencing and thinking about the subtleties of communication, tracing the threads of connection, finding new identities – these are the sorts of themes that provide common ground where all styles of psychotherapy can inform and enrich each other.

Case studies and vignettes

These are a mixture of fictional creations that are shaped through the writers' experiences, and composite characters are drawn from a number of client examples. Chapters 7 and 10 use anonymous descriptions of people who have given their permission for the material to be used in this way.

Contributors

Elizabeth Ashby is a lead art psychotherapist and supervisor who has worked for many years in the NHS with disadvantaged client groups, and she is also in private practice. She is currently engaged in PhD research on the impact of the work on the art psychotherapist, reflecting her concerns about therapist well-being and self care, and has written about her work with clients.

Tim Bray manages a family mediation and family counselling service in Herefordshire. He is a BACP accredited counsellor. His first 'career' was as an outdoor pursuits instructor, working with children in London. He continues to use the natural environment as an agent for personal development and growth.

Caroline Hall worked as a psychologist in the prison service before moving to York University, where she was head of the counselling service. Her publications include *Getting Down to Writing: A Students' Guide to Overcoming Writer's Block*. Now retired, she pursues a wide range of interests but is particularly focused on developing links between community-based art therapies.

Angela Harrison is a music therapist and viola player, formerly of the Hallé Orchestra. She leads the team for the North Yorkshire Music Therapy Centre, a registered charity dedicated to improving access to music therapy for people with illness or disability. Angela has presented at national, European and international conferences and is an executive officer for the professional organization for music therapists in the UK.

Chris Rose is a group psychotherapist, supervisor and consultant working formerly in the NHS, now in private practice and higher education. As teacher, group facilitator, course director and staff consultant, she has extensive counselling and psychotherapy training experience. She writes on group work in *Therapy Today* and is the author of *The Personal Development Group: The Student's Guide*.

Tom Warnecke is a relational body psychotherapist and supervisor with a private practice in London. He has worked in community mental health services and facilitates psychotherapy training courses in various settings. His publications include journal papers and a chapter about

xiv   *Notes on Contributors*

somatic-relational perspectives on borderline personality disorder in *Contemporary Body Psychotherapy: The Chiron Approach* edited by Linda Hartley. He is a vice chair of UKCP.

Richard Worsley is a psychotherapist and supervisor, who works in the counselling service at the University of Warwick. He has a background in counsellor training and he has also been an Anglican parish priest. He is interested in group work, process in counselling, the philosophy and spirituality of counselling, integration, practitioner research and philosophical theology. He has published a number of books in these areas.

1

Self Awareness in Psychotherapy and Counselling

Chris Rose

Our attempts in the twenty-first century to understand ourselves are part of a long tradition of enquiry that stretches through generations, cultures and disciplines. We humans have been fascinated with ourselves for a long time, although the ways in which the self has been understood and expressed has changed with context. This book is concerned with a particular aspect of this endeavour, which is to be found in the theories and practices of psychotherapy and counselling. For many in contemporary society, psychotherapy and counselling have become the context of their search for self awareness and understanding.

When we encounter situations and people that destabilize our certainties about who we are, we need new ways of understanding and being that can encompass these experiences. Psychotherapy and counselling have the potential to provide some of these richer definitions through the particular forms of relationships that they offer. However, psychotherapy is not just the place in which others come to learn about themselves, but where therapists too will discover new things about who they are and how they react.

There are types and models of psychotherapy and counselling that range from short-term solution-focused therapy to long-term psychodynamic explorations of the self and the nature of human existence. The labels 'psychotherapy' and 'counselling' are used interchangeably in some settings, while in others distinctions are made in training requirements and competence to work with particular client groups. This book is concerned with all those therapies that consider the relationship between the client and the therapist to be a key factor in therapeutic change, whether identified as counselling or psychotherapy. The commonality that is relevant here is the recognition that the person of the therapist has a responsibility to understand their own contribution to the therapeutic relationship. Those versions that see the therapist as an expert who can diagnose and treat problems using a range of techniques do not usually insist that the therapist examines herself or himself at any depth, viewing the techniques as the vehicle of change. However it is impossible to rinse the human interactive element from any therapy that is delivered by people rather than computers or self help manuals.

All relationships are processes occurring between people, joint creations that cannot be adequately conceptualized as the exclusive responsibility of either party, and therapeutic relationships are no exception. The client 'self' and the therapist 'self' jointly create the therapeutic relationship and its outcomes, which is why it is vital to understand as much as possible about both participants in the interaction. As psychotherapists and counsellors, our own capacities to listen and respond are related to our experiences as members of a particular gender, class, race, family, culture and society; all these things shape the emotions we experience and the thoughts that we have. They shape the relationships we can offer and inhabit. It is not possible to leave behind who we are as we walk into the counselling room and take our seat. However much we may try to disguise this, the person of the therapist is embedded in the professional role. This is why it is so important that self awareness is seen not as the exclusive responsibility of the client, but as an integral part of both training and continuing professional development for the therapist.

Becoming a competent counsellor or psychotherapist involves a continuing commitment to explore and struggle with ourselves within the training context and beyond. This book sets out to provide some resources and support for those who are prepared in their personal and professional lives to explore their own selves, whether they be students or qualified counsellors and psychotherapists. Although its main focus is upon trainees, it is not confined exclusively to this stage. The level of qualification is not necessarily a measure of personal growth, and in this area there is always more to be discovered. Self awareness and personal development are part of the ongoing project of being a competent therapist.

The difficulties of developing awareness

Learning about ourselves presents some particular challenges. There is no reliable body of wisdom that we can consult that will explain definitively who we are, because it appears that it is 'ourselves' who are holding much of the relevant information. At the same time, most of us acknowledge that others are able to see aspects of ourselves that we are unable to glimpse, and hold different and varied types of information about who we are. Any answers, if that is how we label them, are multi-faceted, fluid constructs revealed through our encounters, relationships, beliefs, imagination and physicality.

There is a widespread recognition that we can be motivated by hidden, contradictory and complex needs. The idea that there is something happening 'behind the scenes' has been intellectually developed in various formats, such as out-of-awareness or the unconscious mind or process. In part, developing self awareness can be thought of as the struggle to bring into conscious awareness that which has been previously out of sight or on the 'edge of awareness'. This can be experienced as a realization that is simultaneously fresh but familiar – as if you knew something all the time but have only just recognized that you knew it; or it can be strikingly new and reveal some aspects of self previously completely hidden from you. The book suggests different avenues through which to access these previously unknown or obscured aspects of self.

The view of ourselves that we bring as adults into psychotherapy and counselling is usually well established and familiar. However much we intellectually assent to the proposition that we need to explore and develop as people, it is emotionally challenging to let go of our certainties and look afresh at how we interact, move, speak and think. This contributes towards making personal development one of the most difficult aspects of counselling and psychotherapy training.

In addition, it is a considerable challenge to provide the most appropriate context for this sort of learning within an educational institution that has other priorities. Most psychotherapy and counselling models assert the crucial importance of offering clients a containing relational context within which to learn and grow. However much effort teaching staff may make to provide this, training courses by their nature involve marked assignments, scrutinized and judged performances and covert if not open competition. We would not expect our clients to find these environments conducive to personal risk taking, so perhaps we should not be surprised when despite demonstrable academic learning, some students struggle with the challenge of exploring their own selves.

Training staff are often caught between a rock and a hard place, with the demands of the educational institution dominating the personal development curriculum. Criteria for marking an assignment can be made clear, transparent and comprehensible to the wider institution, whereas assessments of personal growth can be challenged as lacking 'objectivity' and thereby deemed invalid. Confidentiality plays another complex role in the training context and there are often uncertainties about the status of disclosures. Above all, there is a fundamental tension between the requirement that students meet set criteria and their need to experiment in safe and confidential spaces.

This compounds the difficulties in both challenging and supporting students in their personal work. The vehicles that may be offered for this task, such as supervision, personal therapy, experiential groups and learning journals, are all potentially valuable but can be consciously and unconsciously subverted into exercises that have to be got through rather than exciting opportunities for genuine personal learning. This book offers resources to support both trainers and students in this challenging environment.

So what is a self?

In developing self awareness, what is it that we are trying to develop? The book identifies four key characteristics that will form the basis for exploration.

1. Self as open to change

Psychotherapy and counselling are not just concerned with issues of identity. They are also simultaneously wrestling with ideas about change. Discovering more about 'who we are' is not an endpoint, for that would imply that there is a static and fixed answer to the question. Understanding and experience can lead to the possibility of doing things differently, of looking afresh, of moderating engrained responses, and of enhancing our relationships. We can behave differently, think differently and feel differently. This is not to imply that we can wipe out our 'selves' and start with a blank sheet, but to acknowledge that every aspect is not rigidly held in place and some have the capacity to transform. This is the hope that psychotherapists and counsellors hold out, in various ways, to those who come through their doors, and it is important to keep it in mind for ourselves also.

2. Self as contextual

Although humans have been asking ourselves 'Who am I?' for a very long time, we have failed to come up with a definitive answer, despite an enormous amount of thinking, writing and research. There is always more to say because the question itself, although apparently simple, is either enormously complex or impossible to answer. Particular communities or groups may assert that they have the answer, but in the contemporary world the alternative versions are impossible to eradicate. Ideas and images flow around the global network while huge movements of people destabilize certainties and securities. This is the historical and political context in which we now ask the question 'Who am I?', and like all previous contexts, it shapes the answers that we can find.

The context within which the question is asked and answered is an integral part of the exploration. 'Who am I?' becomes an intelligible question only when other accompanying qualifications are made clear. Questions such as 'Who am I at this moment?' or 'Who wants to know?' and 'For what purpose?' help us to comprehend the context of the enquiry. If you are asked 'What sort of person are you?' in a job interview or by a loved one, the responses will be shaped by the setting. This not only involves the immediate physical and psychological environment but encompasses the cultural, historical, economic and socio-political landscape within which this question has meaning.

It is a central argument of this book that we cannot separate ourselves from the societies, cultures and times within which we live. If we are to learn anything about ourselves, it can only be within those contexts. The more we can grasp of the context, the better our understanding of ourselves. The big picture involves political systems, historical movements, physical environments, intellectual currents and globalized economies. The personal level involves our relationships with others and the communicative network that connects us together. The bigger and the smaller picture are intimately interwoven in ways that are not always readily recognized, and this forms part of the exploration ahead.

3. Self as multiple

Whenever we try to examine our selves, we look for what we believe should be there, relying upon inherited and often unexamined maps to guide us. One of the key aspects of this book is its treatment of the self as multiple rather than unitary, but it is important for every reader to arrive at their own definitions rather than to uncritically accept what is presented. Certainly within Western European popular culture, there is a view of the 'self' as unitary, with consistent patterns of emotion, thought and behaviour. This owes much to the persisting influence of Descartes, in whose thinking the self became an intellectual unit distinct from the body.

We value consistency in our relationships because it enables us to make reasonable predictions of present and future behaviours.

We need reliable repeating factors that can be taken for granted while we concentrate on negotiating the unknown and unpredictable situations. We need stability, containment, attachment and security. Without regularities and patterns we are lost, for they represent the marks on the map that enable us to navigate through life.

As always, there is another side. However essential they are to our survival, reliability and consistency are not enough. We need innovation, imagination, creativity – new solutions to old problems, new pathways, excitement and stimulation. Here is an essential paradox of the human condition: we have apparently contradictory needs and desires. Immediately this is acknowledged, the image of the unitary self becomes problematic.

Most people recognize that they do not think, act or feel the same in every situation. They might describe this using the concept of 'role', as it has become a widely familiar way of thinking about self and other. We are like actors, with different parts in different scenes and productions. We may play the clown when we are out with friends, the peacekeeper in the family and the serious administrator in the office. As the scene changes with time and circumstance, so do our roles.

Inseparable from the idea of role is that of the actor. Are we just a collection of roles or is there someone, the real person, who is performing these roles? Is there a distinctive 'I' that wears various costumes according to the situation, and that can be revealed back in the dressing room? Is there a self that could be described as 'core', or 'true', or 'authentic' – or perhaps as 'spirit' or 'soul'? Or are we missing the point in thinking of any of these as either/or options?

Later in the book we will look more closely at ways in which the 'self' has been conceptualized, particularly within the dominant models of psychotherapy and counselling. Both the humanistic and psychodynamic traditions have well-developed arguments supporting the idea of the self as multiple rather than unitary. At this point it is enough to reconsider the question of 'Who am I?' and to play with a wider range of enquiries, such as 'Who am I in this context?' or 'Who am I when relating to this person?' Freeing ourselves from the straitjacket of trying to be, or thinking we are, just one sort of person is a useful place to start in developing our awareness of self.

4. No self without other

Just as there can be no 'baby' without 'mother', there is no 'self' without 'other'. In exploring and developing our understanding of the multiple aspects of our self, we are inescapably enmeshed with other selves and their multiplicity. Although self awareness might sound like a solitary pursuit, it relies upon others. To become aware of oneself involves becoming aware of all the others who have been and who are a part of us, for we are created in and through relationships. Even the hermit is a member of some family, tribe, culture, religion, historical and environmental context; there is really no escape from others. Before a baby is born, it is a member of some social grouping – family, class, society, race and culture. It has no control over any of these aspects that will form the medium, like amniotic fluid, within which it will develop.

Western European/North American culture promotes and values the individual above the social. It values autonomy and independence, making those within it less able or willing to see the ways in which we are formed by and dependent upon the relational context. We can be less appreciative too of the ways in which we are in our turn forming and shaping others. When we encounter cultures that prioritize family, tribe, clan or community, we may view this attitude as less 'developed' than our own ways of understanding. However, once we begin to question the propaganda that elevates self worth, self sufficiency, self determination, self possession and preoccupation, we start to see its limits. We also see that it serves particular political and economic ends. Certainly, it is true that we want some measure of control over our lives. We rightly fear domination, incorporation and annihilation, but we also dread isolation. We fear imprisonment but want to be securely held. We need to feel attached, to belong and to experience intimacy.

The self develops in and through relationships, and self awareness grows in the same way. It is a fundamental wisdom of counselling and psychotherapy that our clients and patients need relationship and dialogue in order to discover more about themselves and their predicaments. Personal understanding requires personal conversation. If this is true, it applies to all of us, not just those who find themselves with the label of client or patient. Most importantly, we need recognition and validation from others to have confidence in our own self description.

The emphasis upon the other does not imply that there is no space for solitude, in the sense of being alone with ourselves. It does ask questions, however, about the nature of that experience and the extent to which we can exist outside of the framework of others. Solitude can be many things. It can be a noisy internal space populated by the voices and images of others. It can be experienced as desperate aloneness or a place of deep and comforting silence. A quiet reflective walk in the

countryside may induce a powerful sense of isolation or one of profound connection. Either way, through absence or presence, the other
remains central to our experience.

The book

The book presents an image of the self that is shaped by the themes
discussed above. It is a self that is multiple, capable of change, interde-
pendent on others and comprehensible only within its varied contexts.
The book is written by practising psychotherapists and counsellors from
different fields who share both this vision of the self and the belief that
psychotherapeutic practice requires commitment on the part of the
therapist to develop their self awareness. We also share the belief that
experiential learning is the most powerful tool in increasing our own
understanding of who we are, which presents a challenge to us as writers. As far as we have been able, we have presented the material in a
conversational style, because that is exactly what we hope to achieve –
a conversation with the reader within which it is possible to explore
and take risks. All of us – clients, patients, therapists, trainees and readers of this book – require certain common conditions in order to move
beyond familiar narratives about ourselves into new areas. We strive to
offer a non-judgemental, containing yet challenging context where in
complete confidentiality readers can explore themselves. Each chapter
is rather like a workshop, with discussion and exercises to provoke and
encourage a personal response.

The book begins with an examination of various ways that the self
has been conceptualized in contemporary models of psychotherapy and
counselling. The focus is upon different lenses or perspectives that are
applied to the self in psychodynamic and humanistic theories that form
the dominant models within training. The reader is invited to reflect
upon their own underlying assumptions about self and personhood in
order to lay a framework for the further explorations ahead.

Subsequent chapters are based around different modes of counselling
and psychotherapy, each corresponding to a particular field or style. If
we consider these pathways to be helpful in enabling clients to see, feel
and think about themselves more clearly then they must be valid ways
in which to see ourselves as therapists more clearly also.

Chapter 3 is concerned with our reactions and responses to other
people and what can be learnt from these. Looking at our capacities
as humans to comprehend each other's experience, it suggests that the
concept of resonance is a useful way of thinking about these processes.

The chapter goes on to examine the major divisions within society, attempting to recognize the frameworks that shape our relationships in powerful and often unconscious ways. Difference and similarity are discussed and framed in the context of group memberships, again emphasizing the fundamental group nature of social existence. This has clear relevance to the client/therapist encounter and is demonstrated through examples with invitations to the reader to consider her or his own responses.

Chapter 4 builds on this through focusing upon conversation as the means by which we relate to and comprehend ourselves and others. In particular, it discusses the types of conversation that are available in the context of training, in supervision, personal therapy and especially in the personal development group. Conversations with others teach us many things while building the capacity to talk with ourselves; learning to recognize characteristic internal voices can play a highly significant role in the development of self awareness. The ways in which these voices or characters communicate is examined through the metaphor of the internal group, where a facilitative voice takes a key role in establishing creative internal dialogues.

In the following chapter, the focus moves to the opportunities for self awareness that can be found in the process of writing. Although considered 'talking' therapies, counselling and psychotherapy are heavily dependent upon the written word, whether in journals, case studies, notes or emails. Picking up on the earlier discussion about internal dialogues and internal groups, Caroline Hall explores the potential for developing self awareness that the written word can offer.

Angela Harrison draws upon examples from her experiences as a musician and music therapist, writing about the ways in which music of all kinds is able to expand our awareness of self and others. She explores the ways in which the music we hear and are attracted to can provide insights into aspects of the self, and how our own music making can be a powerful means of self expression.

Elizabeth Ashby continues the self exploration through the use of visual imagery. She writes about the power of the visual to provide a way of reflecting on our selves and our lives through bringing into consciousness areas that were previously out of awareness. Images can convey and contain powerful emotions in the context of both individual client work and also supervision. Visual imagery also offers a means of self expression and the opportunity to play.

Tom Warnecke explores the body as an agency for self discovery, exploring aspects of mind–body, psyche–soma relations in order to develop our appreciation of the essential embodiment of self. He describes the ways in which we speak with our bodies, resonating with the presence, actions and expressions of others, and illustrates this with an extended vignette. Our abilities to relate and develop intimacy are deepened by the awareness of our bodies and their felt senses.

We are not only embodied selves, but embedded in an environment. The next chapter takes the form of an interview in which Tim Bray talks about his powerful relationship with the natural environment, and the ways in which this has enabled him to reflect upon himself. The interview questions can be used by readers to explore their own relationship with the natural world, and develop their awareness of the connections between this and other significant relationships.

'There must be more than this.' In the following chapter, Richard Worsley invites us to consider the transcendent in both religious and secular contexts. He sees the transcendent as an aspect of self that can be heard particularly through metaphor and narrative. He argues that if we cannot hear this in ourselves, we fail to hear it in our clients. Transcendence is related to our capacity to genuinely encounter the other, which is itself integral to the counselling relationship.

In summary, the book journeys through our relationships, with both individuals and groups, the written word, music, visual images, the body, the natural environment and transcendence. All of these areas are rich fields for exploration that offer different ways to access and develop parts of the self. Although the authors share a common vision and purpose, they have their own distinctive voices that will provoke varied responses. Each chapter invites the reader into a unique reader/author relationship that creates further opportunities for developing self awareness.

Setting out

There are many possible reactions to the book, and some are more helpful in the pursuit of self awareness than others. Before going further, it will be useful to reflect upon the different types of responses that the book may draw out.

Repetition, re-experiencing, ruminating

The phrase 'thinking about' can have a variety of meanings, and in the context of this book it is important to distinguish this from ruminating. Although ruminating may be used to mean no more than thinking deeply, it has another less benign meaning that describes a cyclic, repetitive process of bringing to mind and replaying past hurts and grievances. It is important to distinguish this from the creative process that thinking can represent.

If the material that is being replayed is traumatic, repeatedly going over incidents can be a recurring source of fear and anguish. Our ideas about the therapeutic value of re-experiencing emotional trauma have changed through time and if in the search for self awareness we find ourselves reliving painful experiences, then at best this is unhelpful and at worst it is damaging. These situations may require the support of an experienced and qualified 'other' to facilitate a creative resolution. If it is to lead to any development of self awareness, self reflection requires different ways of communicating with ourselves that can get beyond repetition and re-experiencing.

Communicating with ourselves

To learn about ourselves we cannot avoid some form of communication with others or with ourselves. But if we talk to ourselves, who is answering? And who is asking the question? Perhaps we think of an 'I' who is talking to a 'myself'? Or perhaps we are already alert to a range of possible selves who will have something to contribute to an internal conversation. Paying attention to the subtleties and tones of our internal communications is one of the most powerful keys to self awareness. We experience in many different forms, but to be able to think about what the experience might mean or the impact that it has had on us, we are going to need language. There is much more to say later in the book about our capacity to talk with ourselves in different styles and voices.

Imagination and creativity

Whatever route is chosen, it is clear that developing self awareness is a scientific rational project only insofar as we are scientific, rational people. There is too much of human life that remains unknown or not understood for us to rely entirely upon scientific enquiry. Imagination and creativity are some of the great characteristics of human life, and they have the potential to expand our awareness beyond our immediate consciousness. The ability to create, in whatever medium, can enable us to push beyond the concrete and the known into new understandings and experiences. Creativity comes in many shapes and styles, and one of the challenges in developing self awareness is to uncover and attend to whatever form it takes in our own lives.

One important way to learn from this book is to try out the activities suggested and allow yourself to play. It is perhaps tempting to just read them and pass on, but there is so much more to be learnt from actually engaging with them. You, the reader, will have unique responses that are the essential ingredients of your own self awareness. It is a valuable opportunity to catch sight of your selves from different and hopefully surprising angles. Points for reflection are presented like this.

Points for reflection

You might like to keep a record of your thoughts and discoveries as you read through this book. It could be in the form of a journal, a painting, a scrapbook, a blog, a new file – whatever form attracts you. It may be drawn, painted, sculpted or written, or it may be a collection of things, sketches, scribbles or photos.

It is a creative project crafted by you, about you. It could provide valuable material for any personal journal that your training course may require.This project, however, is completely confidential, and never needs to be discussed or shared with anyone else unless you choose to do so. It can become your partner in the self exploration that lies ahead.

Letting go

There will be times when we need to stop thinking, insofar as we are able to. Letting go of a question or dilemma can be just as important as tenaciously pursuing it. We have the ability to process material while it is not in our direct focus, so that we can 'sleep on' a dilemma, for example, and awake with new inspiration. There will be an important part to play for the dreams we might have too, as well as the day-time reveries. Material for self reflection comes as much from intimations and fleeting glimpses as from direct and sustained examination.

Throughout this entire endeavour we do well to recognize that there are limits to our capacity to develop self awareness. In trying to understand more about ourselves we will find that our certainties become less secure: we know less than we thought we did, but more about the extent of the unknown. Developing self awareness is a process, not an achievement. It describes an ongoing interest in ourselves and others whereby paradoxically, the more attention we pay to understanding ourselves the less self important we become. It is a challenging and serious task, but it is also fun, creative and liberating.

2
Thinking about the Self

Chris Rose and Richard Worsley

There is a long history of questioning what it might mean to be a self and many different theories have been put forward. The reader who asks that same question draws upon an intellectual heritage that will inevitably shape the ideas and concepts that are used; very few of us, if any, can think entirely new thoughts. We are always building or rebuilding upon the foundations laid by others, who in their turn did the same.

The ways in which we think about the self will define and shape our understanding of self awareness. The previous chapter, for example, presented four ways of looking at the self that have shaped my own ideas and therefore influenced this book. This chapter invites you to examine your ideas about what a self might be, and to consider some of the contributions others have made to defining self hood. In order for this not to be constrained by my own ways of thinking, I have invited Richard Worsley to share in the writing.

Here we look at five different perspectives that can be identified as influential in thinking about questions of self in the context of counselling and psychotherapy. The aim is to demonstrate a process or way of approaching theories of self, rather than to provide a comprehensive account. That would be a monumental task, already undertaken elsewhere, which the reader might like to investigate at some point (e.g., Burkett 2008; Taylor 1989).

The five perspectives or lenses through which we look at theory are multiple, narrative, organismic, ethical and relational. It is not an exhaustive list, of course, but represents some important intellectual strands within psychotherapy and counselling, inevitably reflecting the dominant North American and European cultural perspective in this area. None of the lenses stand alone or offer a complete definition of the self; rather it is in the dialogues and tensions between these various strands that we find the most satisfying understandings of self hood.

Theories are valuable in developing self awareness in so far as they can illuminate our experience. In the interplay between what we think we know and what others claim to know there is room for genuine learning. To demonstrate this, the chapter is organized around a fictitious trainee counsellor, who is asked to think about herself. The material she provides can then be looked at through the five various lenses. This also provides a model for the reader to apply to their own self description.

Carmen

Carmen is 36, training as a counsellor on a course with an integrative model. This is how she responds when asked to tell us about herself.

'First and foremost I am a mother. My closest relationship is with my 18-year-old daughter, Carrie. I was only 18 myself when she was born, although I'd been determined not to have a baby so young, just like my own mother. I hope I'm not like her in any other ways. She was a cruel, selfish woman as far as I'm concerned.

I have a good steady relationship with my partner, Paul. We've been together for six years now. He's partially sighted so I do a lot of the practical things in our relationship. I suppose I am the one in charge, but he's happy with that and we get on fine. He's a gentle man, not like my stepfather or my granddad. He and Carrie get on well too, which is really important. Sometimes I get quite envious of their relationship.

I never had that sort of father myself; in fact I never even met him. All I know is that he and my mum were at school together. She was 15 and he was 16, Afro-Caribbean and very good looking. She said his family moved away and she never saw him any more. She wanted an abortion but my grandparents wouldn't let her – they're Catholics. Otherwise I wouldn't be here.

The other important person has always been my Nana. She brought me up, really, and I am very fond of her. When she had a stroke in her 70s it pulled me up short and I stopped messing about with drink and drugs and took life seriously. In a funny way it was the best thing that could have happened to me, though I wouldn't be saying that if she hadn't recovered. I went to college and did an access course, and worked really hard to get a place at university. My Nana was so proud of me. She has always been interested in things, reading and learning, not like anyone else in my family. She's in a home now, still quite lively in her mind and I see her every week. Granddad died years ago when I was 13. Nana says he was fond of me, but he was very stern and I was quite scared of him. He did once make me a wooden boat, I remember, to sail in the bath.

It was only when I went to school that I realized how different I looked. It was a very small Catholic primary school and there were only two of us with dark skin. I've had a lot of racial abuse in my time and never found it easy to fit in. I remember that when my grandparents used to take me to the Irish club I stood out like a sore thumb. It was only when I was at university in my twenties that I found a group of friends, some of them mixed race, where I felt reasonably comfortable. But I'm still not good in groups.

I'm never sure with people. Usually I'm very quiet but then I can be very lively, joking and talking loudly. Then I worry that I'm too noisy and taking over, so I withdraw again. I've got one really close friend, Jeannie. She's half-Irish too, kind and funny. We had a lot of ups and downs in the early days but now we can fall out and still be best mates. I know I can be a pretty angry person at times, especially if I'm fighting for someone's rights, like at work. I work in a social housing unit, and I can be very tough if I need to be. Justice is really important to me and I will fight hard for it.

Carrie and I have our rows too. She's got a temper like me, but I still love her to bits and would do anything for her. I never want her to feel the things that I did when I was small. My mum married when I was 4 and then for a while I lived with her and Rory, my stepfather. He was a horrible loud-mouthed thug, and I was terrified of him. When my half-brothers came along I was supposed to look after them, and I was only a kid myself. In the end the social services got involved and I went back to live with my grandparents.

That was a long time ago. I've worked hard and have got a good family now, and I'm looking forward to the future. There's some optimistic bit of me that never gives up even when things are tough.'

Points for reflection

Having read Carmen's account, try writing your own of about the same length (800 words). Notice what is included and what is omitted. Then look at your self description through the various lenses below.

The multiple perspective

As this perspective thinks of selves as created through multiple experiences of relating, it shares much of its theoretical base with the relational lens. This has its roots in the object relations tradition, developed in the works of Fairbairn (1952, 54), Winnicott (1953, 65) and Kernberg (1976, 80), for example. However, not all relational theorists work with the perspective of multiplicity. Some (e.g., Kohut 1977) envisage a self that has some form of core or authentic self. Although much of this book is written from the multiple self perspective, it is important to explore this divergent view, as most people would describe themselves initially as a unitary rather than a multiple self.

Carmen, for example, thinks of herself as possessing an interior unitary self, unique, private and impossible to really know or describe. She acknowledges that she can behave differently according to circumstance, recognizing, for example, an angry Carmen, and a compassionate Carmen; but for her, these are all expressions of a unitary self. Deep down, she sees herself as the same person.

The words we choose to articulate our sense of self are, as any therapist knows, highly significant. Carmen's language points us in the direction of looking beneath the surface to find some essential core. In this she follows a long tradition of conceptualizing the self as buried deep within us. The Romantic ideal of a natural self that could be uncovered from layers of social conditioning and the Freudian vision of a powerful underlying energy threatening to break through the civilized veneer are both examples of this sort of topography. They describe the self through images of place, surface and depth. To understand the self in these spatial terms is always to go deeper. Self is reified, unitary and continuous, hidden away in the innermost recess.

The multiple perspective, on the other hand, argues that self is created in interaction with others, and it is an intersubjective process that shapes our experience of the world. We become who we are in the context of multiple relationships set within a historical and socio-political context. The self is a process, intra-personal and interpersonal, rather than some thing or place located within us (Mitchell 1993). Even our experience of our own bodies is given meaning through the cultural, social and personal context that we find ourselves in. From the flow of these multiple experiences we learn patterns or constellations of responses, emotions and beliefs that make up who we are. Instead of looking deep within to find a space or place, the multiple self lens is concerned with time and context; through this lens we cannot see a unitary self that sits at the heart of our being.

This is not to say that there is no place for authenticity. Carmen recognizes that when she is at work she is experienced as a competent and forceful person, and that both reflects and is a reflection of how she generally experiences herself in this context. There she can be interested, passionate and fully absorbed with no sense of not being 'herself'.

Then she can be at home, cooking and singing in the kitchen with her daughter, or sitting in tears with Jeannie, fearful of the future. There is no sense, either for Carmen or others involved, that these very different experiences are in any way superficial or inauthentic. Instead of an 'authentic self', there are experiences of authenticity. The multiple self perspective moves from a view of self as spatial, to one that is temporal. The self is created moment to moment through interactions with people and contexts that can be variously experienced as consciously false at one extreme, to vital and authentic at the other.

Understanding more of this process does not change Carmen's experience of herself as a continuous unitary self. It serves to clarify more the process by which multiple selves may be created, but there remains the challenge of explaining the sense that most of us have of being one self rather than many. From the perspective of the multiple self, this experience of unity is formed though the capacity to self-reflect and create meaning (Mitchell 1993; Bromberg 1996). It is through thinking about what we have experienced that we construct a seemingly unified self, selecting and editing the myriad impressions and emotions that attend each day into a reasonably coherent narrative. Our lived experience is often chaotic and confused and it is only afterwards that we can 'make sense' of what has happened. This is a vital and necessary aspect of self that enables us to function, holding together the multiplicity of self. It is one of the features of multiple personality disorder, for example, that there is no narrative that weaves together the different selves, leaving them in isolation from each other.

It is only in the last twenty years that person-centred theory has done justice to the multiplicity of self. Carl Rogers' view was mainly of a unitary self, deeply influenced by his foundational metaphor of the self as a (single) biological organism. John Rowan brought to this new thinking about what he termed sub-personalities, and researched this in groups and workshops (Rowan 1990). More recently, Mearns and Thorne (2000) have put forward the theory of configurations of the self.

Different configurations represent different patterns of feeling and behaviour that have been introjected. These are catalogued and defensively protected by something like a firewall in order to reduce tension and incongruence between them. In addition, these configurations are constructs in that the person may experience them, address them and name them. The purpose of this, both in everyday life and in therapy, is to improve communication between configurations so as to reduce incongruence, and hence the need for the defensive wall. This version of the multiple self lens might also point to the angry Carmen and the compassionate Carmen. At first, Carmen might presume a unitary self and these adjectives as mere attributes of the behaviour of this self. However the configurations have characteristic attitudes, feelings and behaviours which do not belong to the whole. She can become able to recognize and express these differences, to engage and negotiate with them, and to develop further configurations to bring about a more integrated set of selves.

Here in this book the multiple lens perspective is expressed and developed through the metaphor of the internal group. Each version of self is portrayed as a member of a group, in which the process of creating a communicative network represents growth and integration. If one member is able to develop the capacity to facilitate the group, this can provide and stimulate the vital reflective and containing function that makes sense of what is happening. This voice or character can help generate dialogue between the different group members, provide an overall view and assist the creation of a meaningful narrative. At this point the lens of multiple self brings into view the narrative perspective.

The narrative perspective

The starting point here is to observe that our identity constitutes itself in the language we use about ourselves. Language is a means of assembling and enacting our identities (Etherington 2007; Mc Leod 1997). Language not only expresses things, but it enacts things (Austin 1962). In some cultures for instance, the words 'I divorce you' actually are constitutive of the divorce.

Our use of language then builds up the narratives we have about ourselves. The most influential thinker in this area has perhaps been the French philosopher, Paul Ricoeur (Kearney 2004; Muldoon 2002; Ricoeur 1978; Ricoeur 1998). He points out that narratives do not express a single, literal truth about the self. Rather, truth is pointed to, imprecisely, by the matrix of narratives we have about ourselves, and in particular by the tension, the differences, between the many narratives we have about ourselves. Ricoeur's key point is that only technical language has a single meaning. It is what he calls univocal. However, language at its most human is not univocal. It both carries the possibility of multiple meanings and is the instrument of the creation of meaning (Muldoon 2002: chs 3 and 4). Thus, the stories we tell about ourselves, either inwardly or outwardly, constitute for us our felt-meaning of ourselves and our existence.

Therapists will be all too familiar with hearing clients' narratives and being surprised by the diversity and at times the contradiction between them. Therapy itself can be thought of as the retelling of our narratives until they work in a different way. They are rarely complete and systematic, like a well-crafted short story or novel. They are incomplete. They are sometimes wholly unacknowledged, at least until another person points to them. In listening to life narratives, it is sometimes as much a construct of the listener as the teller of the narratives as to what makes up a single story. It seems to me that tone and feeling are as important as coherence in a story. Holmes (1999) suggests that there is a strong relationship between the type and style of stories we tell about ourselves and our early experiences of attachment.

Carmen seems to set out a raft of possible narratives with her opening comment that she is *first and foremost* a mother. What is the story here? It can of course be the story of the pleasure of motherhood, and it is likely to be that in part. It is also, it feels, the story of an intense dyad, of two and not three people. It is a relationship in which Carmen strives to be more like her Nana than her mother. Even the words Nana and mother have feelings attached, perhaps.

I say perhaps because all narratives are speculative, certainly for the listener and sometimes for the teller. We can never be sure what things mean. Ricoeur differentiates between narratives of suspicion, which point to hidden, sometimes denied, meanings, and narratives of affirmation which point to future and open meaning (Kearney 2004: 26–29). We can speculate as to whether a narrative is one of suspicion or of affirmation. We might even speculate that one of the points of therapy is to unpack the negativities of suspicion and affirm the future and open narratives.

The story of mothering Carrie is, at least on the surface, one of hope for the future. It is a good and close relationship. It affirms Carrie – or does it? Affirmation is important, but suspicion teaches us to listen, in ourselves as well as others, for the darker aspects of life. Does Carmen, the good mother, *use* Carrie to compensate for what has happened to her? How might that feel to Carrie? The whole point is that we do not know. Narrative-thinking requires humility.

Similarly, we notice that Carmen has struggled to form relationships with men. Paul, her partner, is defined as not like her step-father. His disability seems an important dimension. Just as individuals do not exist in isolation, so narratives also interlock. Carmen and Paul need to work out between them their own story as a couple. Does it work because there is a sort of complementarity or is there hidden conflict?

Suspicion raises questions for affirmation to resolve. Similarly, suspicion would question the affirmation of a better future at the end of her account. Is it genuine or a defence? A parallel deconstruction can also be offered concerning Carmen's commitment to justice. It can be both morally genuine and also a cover for, a projection of, her anger. In a short account lurks a number, perhaps a dozen, of potential narratives. Therapy is sometimes a shared discovery of which ones matter.

One final observation can be made about Carmen through this lens. Ricoeur points out that narrative is closely related to metaphor. In fact he began to think first about metaphor (Ricoeur 1978). In short, metaphor is to the sentence what narrative is to the text. Each embodies a rich ambivalence of meanings; that is to say each is polysemic. I notice that Carmen does not, in her account, use explicit and rich metaphors. Apart from the everyday (but possibly revealing) phrases of 'sticking out like a sore thumb' and 'love her to bits' she offers a very literal story. This might be the product of asking someone for a brief account of herself. However, if on further listening I still heard a poverty of metaphorical thinking, an inability in particular to respond to my use of metaphor, then I would want to think about the processes by which Carmen generates meaning in her life. Is she entrapped in the literal? Does she need, both for herself and her future clients, to learn to think metaphorically? How otherwise will she grasp her own rich and polysemic narratives?

The organismic perspective

'There is some optimistic bit of me that never gives up even when things are tough,' says Carmen. Why do we survive, and at what cost?

The organismic perspective works at a very different level of being human– the biological rather than the linguistic. It takes as its focus the fact that humans are, amongst other things, biological organisms. It is in thinking about ourselves as organisms that some important insights arise. However, within the humanistic tradition of therapy there has also been a range of misunderstandings. Hence it is important to ask both why we survive and what cost our survival has for human living. Survival can be both a triumph and a constriction.

The starting point for thinking about this might well be Carl Rogers' (1963) paper which he gave to the Nebraska Symposium on motivation. Rogers held that there was but a single motivating force operating in the organism, which he termed the actualising tendency.

The biological emphasis of Rogers' thinking means that he is looking for a global constant explanation as to why humans act in particular ways.

He describes the effect upon him of going for a walk along the California coast, where he saw what at first he took to be a colony of miniature palm trees at the water's edge. On closer inspection he found that he was looking at a species of seaweed which had colonised the least hospitable of environments, the edge of the ocean where salt water crashes endlessly onto rocks. He noted that the plants had evolved by forming a trunk-like structure from their fronds, to lift them clear of the water's energy. Systems tend to develop opportunistically, just in the way the seaweed had evolved. So far this is uncontroversial.

However, Rogers postulated that the same actualisation is latent in all humans in terms of their emotional and social well-being. Thus humans are richly adaptive creatures, who can survive by accommodating to the most hostile of environments. Therapy then provides a supportive and reparative environment for further growth.

Two possible misunderstandings strike me as important for thinking about Carmen. Rogers' version of organismic thinking is seen to mean that people were 'essentially good'. This is wildly wrong. If Rogers is right then people are minimally constructive in surviving. It is about adapting to survive (and perhaps prosper). This is not at all about good and bad. Such discourse would fit within the ethical perspective, but not this one.

The second misunderstanding is closely linked to this. Not only are adaptations not 'good' or 'bad', save only in the sense that they serve our need to survive, but not all adaptations are in themselves beneficial to the organism. Thus Carmen has learned to be very wary of men, unless they can be 'controlled'. This can contribute to survival, but it also gets in the way of some good relating. In a similar way, her desire to be a counsellor is admirable for emotional survival. Yet, does compensatory attachment to this role limit her professional formation?

First of all, let us note a health warning about reasoning from evolution. In Rogers' example, all he can observe is the shape of the seaweed, and the nature of the environment. The detailed connection he makes is speculation. We cannot, as David Hume noted, observe causality. With psychological causality there is even more uncertainty. The organismic perspective will generate a number of versions of what might be, and miss others.

However it is theorized, perhaps as lack of unconditional positive regard (Rogers 1951) or perhaps as impoverished attachment (Bowlby

1997), Carmen's major issue seems to be her mother's cruelty, as she perceives it. This attacking behaviour is perhaps Carmen's prime threat. If a mother cannot give the emotional safety a child needs, then one response is to despair. However, Carmen was able to use her Nana's love as a substitute. This did not make her life experience OK. It is still frightening, yet she has enough reassurance that she is love-able to both trust her own growth and to provide better mothering for Carrie. In Winnicott's (1953) terms, Carmen renders Nana's care as good-enough mothering. She can experience Nana as an adequate holding space for her. She, after all, saved her from being aborted. That is no small thing! Whatever the literal truth, this is a powerful metaphor, that Nana can hold some of the most primitive parts of Carmen.

What about men? The first man in Carmen's life was her father, yet he was absent. Rory, by contrast, was a major threat, viewed as violence and power out of control. The question – a painful one – is about the nature of her relationship with Paul. He is gentle and therefore safe and that is good. His disability may guarantee that he needs Carmen, but her own words hint at the control she has over him. Is this good, constructive growth, or is it a defence position that needs to be brought into question? If the latter, then it is the case that Paul's version of maleness is not just a good version, but also a rather castrated one. It works as a defence but is it a satisfactory relationship? Is it a cost to pay for immunity to male violence? If so, is it too great a cost?

However simple the organismic perspective might seem at first glance, it can generate a nuanced plethora of questions. The ethical perspective requires a different and more abstract way of thinking of humans.

The ethical perspective

Carmen is training to be a counsellor. During her training she will be learning to think ethically about her practice. In recent years, the British Association for Counselling and Psychotherapy has shifted from decreeing the contents of codes of practice to setting out a framework (BACP 2010), within which to learn to think ethically. Within this is a stress on the moral qualities of a counsellor, and these include empathy, sincerity, integrity, resilience, respect, humility, competence, fairness, wisdom and courage. Counsellors, like other professionals, have to engage with the self as responsible to, and at times for, others. In a fairly obvious sense, the self has to move towards concern for others.

In this section I contend that all humans are essentially ethical beings. That is to say, our being is defective if it centres only on the self. David Brazier (1993) has argued that the key quality of therapy is love, and that in order for the client to be emotionally healthy, she needs to experience herself as a giver as well as receiver of love. In other words humans are altruistic. We need to know that we give and are received. If Brazier is right we carry a concern for the other that we need to honour.

The French philosopher, Emmanuel Levinas, has extended this line of thinking considerably. He argues (Levinas 1969, 1998; Worsley 2006) that we in the west have over the past 3,000 years tended to reduce everything to the Same. By this he means that we see all that there is in terms of our own self. We are philosophically self-centred. The opposite of the Same is the Infinite. By the Infinite Levinas asks us to consider others as profoundly and absolutely different from ourselves. Each individual is constituted by an infinite regression of possibilities which are not like ourselves, are not the Same. There is an infinite capacity to be surprised and astonished by the Other.

However Levinas deduces from the Infinite the metaphor of the face. When we meet the other through gazing into another's face, then we experience the other as Other because she makes a demand upon us that is ethical. It is on these grounds that Peter Schmid (2001) stresses that person-centred therapy (at least) is deeply ethical, because it is profoundly committed to an encounter with the Other. Similarly, Martin Buber (1958) points to I-Thou relating as a consequence of the ethical demands upon us of the Other.

How might this lens help us understand Carmen?

Let us start by imagining that Carmen is sitting in a group with all of the main characters of her life. Each of the people in the group is a real human Other. However, each can also be a projection of part of Carmen's inner world. Each can play a particular role in Carmen's inner drama. The challenge set out by the ethical lens for Carmen is to grow in relationship with these real people as themselves, taking back her projections. This can happen in a number of ways.

I notice that Carrie may be an idealisation of the hurt version of Carmen. If Carmen herself could not get from her mother the love and acceptance she needed, then Carrie can at least do this for her. If this was all there was to the story, then life for Carrie might be oppressive. Living out one's parents' needs is no way to become an individual. However there is a hint that Carmen has already moved beyond this position with Carrie. Carrie is hot-tempered too, like, I imagine, a criticised part of Carmen. Yet, Carmen can accept and love the difficult in Carrie.

I see Carmen's mother as her main challenge. Is she to remain always the rejecting and rejected character? Rejection is centred on the self. That sounds a painful thing to say, and it is not meant to be judgemental. That is just how it works. Can mother be seen as a woman who is also a feeling victim? If Carmen can forgive her mother, then she is beginning to encounter her as an Other and not just a projection. In reality, Carmen may never forgive her mother, but the question is about the possibility of forgiveness.

By contrast, Carmen says that her relationship with Jeannie has moved through hostile conflicts to a stage that allows Jeannie to be different, to not be recruited in Carmen's cause. There are signs that friendship leads Carmen to appreciate the genuinely Other in Jeannie, her alterity.

The process of taking back projections and treating others ethically in the sense of seeing them as decisively other-than-us is also part of Carmen's professional development. Until this step can be made, she risks subordinating clients to her own projections.

The relational perspective is closely linked with the ethical, for both point to being human as being in relationship with others.

The relational perspective

This perspective presents a view of the self as constructed by, and in turn constructing, a relational matrix that develops throughout the lifespan. We are born into contexts and structures of relationships and the self is created in this interactive, co-creative environment. It is a perspective that invites close attention to the phenomenology of moment-to-moment relating, always aware that the context is an integral part of the encounter (Wachtel 2008).

There are different emphases within this relational perspective. Earlier contributors tended to view the mother–baby relationship as laying down a template that determined the shape of all other significant relationships. Bowlby (1969, 1973, 1980), for example, introduced the idea of attachment as a key variable in understanding the self. He and his followers described patterns in the ways in which infants and caregivers attach, which they saw as forming blueprints for subsequent relationships and behaviour.

Winnicott (1965) was also interested in the relationship between mother and infant, and paid particular attention to the responsiveness of the mother to the baby's needs at different stages of development. He saw this as critical for the child to establish a sense of self that was grounded in her or his own experience of the world, rather than a projection of the mother's experience. Stern (1985) further developed this concept of attunement with increasing recognition of the baby's participation and the mutuality of the process.

Heinz Kohut (1977) was interested in the ability to feel energized, alive and connected to others. In his thinking we need an ideal to aspire to, another person to identify with and repeated experiences of being admired and encouraged. These he saw as three crucial relational supports that create a robust self, able to survive setbacks and create a personally meaningful life.

All of these theorists present Carmen with some interesting avenues for self reflection, both as a daughter and as a mother. The ways in which she attaches and enables others to attach to her, her capacity to attune herself to others and her sense of others being attuned to her, and her experiences of encouragement and motivation will all provide differing angles from which to explore her relational self.

So far much of this relational perspective has concentrated upon early experiences. Mitchell (1988) balances this with an appreciation of the significance of other relationships throughout life. Carmen's relationships with Carrie, Paul and Jeannie, for example, are not just re-enactments of earlier relationships. They contain conscious and unconscious aspects of childhood experience but also have new and creative possibilities. He describes the relational web as interpersonal and intrapersonal, arguing that every stimulus or experience is fashioned and organized into a subjective world by an active organism. A self is created like any work of art, from the interplay between an imaginative process and available materials such as relationships and contexts. The materials offer potentials and constraints that the process must work with, but the product is more than the materials.

In this metaphor, the society and culture that is part of everyone's relational context presents us with significant materials that we have to work with. Elias (1991) uses the phrase 'society of individuals' and Burkitt (2008) 'social individuality' to capture this interrelationship. It challenges the popular Western European and North American view that prizes the individual over the group, which is a set of values and beliefs that certain generations in these societies have grown up within and been shaped by.

Carmen's sense that she is 'not good in groups' may be linked to her experience as a mixed-race child in the UK, where she felt that she did not fit comfortably into either the Afro-Caribbean, Irish or English groupings. Racial identity is a key factor in the development of a sense of self, as is gender. Carmen's account contains reference to male indifference, sternness and violence; in contrast, her partner is distinguished by gentleness and submission. There is an implicit set of beliefs and attitudes here about men and women that form a significant strand in Carmen's self identity. Entwined here also is social class, which although not explicit in the account may be inferred. Our memberships of these large societal groups lay the foundations of self, despite a prevalent belief that we are primarily individuals. Our context gives us the materials from which the self is created, and through our interactions and responses we have the opportunities to fashion our own unique version.

The relational perspective continues in a different form in the following chapter, and other perspectives will be encountered as the book progresses. At this stage it is helpful to pause and reflect upon the ways which these five perspectives relate to your own preferred models of self.

Points for reflection

Which of the perspectives of self presented here did you react to, either in agreement or disagreement?

Do any of these accounts of the self resonate with your own? Where are they similar and where are they different? Are there elements here that you feel more or less comfortable with?

What other perspectives would you have suggested?

Do you find yourself attracted to quite differing views, or do you have a clear preference or choice?

The authors here would argue that there is no one perspective that can adequately represent the complex process that we call self. We come closest to that through engaging in dialogue and conversation between the lenses. Being able to tolerate tension and paradox not only gives us a far richer appreciation of what the self might be, but also encourages a more flexible and diverse engagement with others.

Further resources

For more comprehensive discussions on the nature of the self:

Burkitt, I. (2008). *Social Selves: Theories of Self and Society.* 2nd edition. London: Sage.
Taylor, C. (1989). *Sources of the Self: The Making of Modern Identity.* Cambridge: Cambridge University Press.

On the multiple perspective

Mearns, D. and Thorne, B. (2000). *Person-Centred Therapy Today.* London: Sage
Bromberg, P. (1996). 'Standing in the Spaces: The Multiplicity of Self and the Psychoanalytic Relationship'. *Contemporary Psychoanalysis* 3: 2 608–636.

On the organismic perspective

Nobel, D. (2006). *The Music of Life: biology beyond genes.* Oxford: Oxford University Press.
Mearns, D. and Thorne, B. (2007). Person-Centred Counselling in Action. (3rd edition.) London: Sage. Chapter 1.

On the narrative perspective

McLeod, J. (1997). *Narrative and Psychotherapy.* London: Sage.
Holmes, J. (2001) *The Secure Base: Attachment theory and psychotherapy.* Hove, East Sussex: Brunner- Routledge, Chapters 7 and 8.

On the ethical perspective

BACP (2010). Ethical Framework for Good Practice in Counselling and Psychotherapy. Lutterworth: BACP.
Brazier, D. (1993). *The Necessary Condition is Love: Going beyond the self in person-centred therapy.* In D. Brazier (ed.) Beyond Carl Rogers. London: Constable, 72–91.
Worsley, R. (2006). Emmanuel Levinas: Resource and challenge for therapy. *PCEP* 5:3, 208–20.

On the relational perspective

Mitchell, S. (1988). *Relational Concepts in Psychoanalysis: An Integration.* Cambridge, Mass: Harvard University Press.
Wachtel, P. (2008). *Relational Theory and the Practice of Psychotherapy.* New York; Guilford.

Finally, a book that touches upon all these perspectives through a psychoanalytic lens:

Molino A. (ed). (1996). *Elaborate Selves: Reflections and Reveries of Christopher Bollas, Michael Eigen, Polly Young-Eisendrath, Samuel and Evelyn Laeuchli and Marie Coleman Nelson.* Worcester, UK; Clunie Press.

3
Developing through Relationships with Others

Chris Rose

This chapter looks at what we can learn about ourselves through our relationships with others, beginning an exploration that continues in different ways throughout the book. The people that we encounter and the contexts within which we meet them offer endless opportunities to discover more about ourselves. Every encounter that elicits a response has the potential to expand our awareness of self and other. The response is the starting point, like an arrow on a map marking 'you are here'. The map is not the exclusive property of one person but is fundamentally relational – a mutual exchange that in the search for self awareness can be captured and explored.

How we respond

Before we set out, it is worth reflecting upon the nature of our responses. We may respond with a bodily sensation, a felt sense, a thought, an emotion, an image, an association or any combination of these reactions. All of these provide potentially useful material and it is not necessary to attribute higher value to one rather than another. What is more important is to recognise that none are absolute, and that our responses are part of the cultural, social and familial landscape that we inhabit.

For example, the language that is available to identify, describe and communicate emotion is, like all language, a socially constructed system. In other words, the ways in which we recognise, express and describe feeling are all shaped by the language community we grow up in. Despite the commonalities of human experience, different languages construct different types of emotional landscapes. These are embedded in the particular society, shaped by social class, status, gender, sexuality and so forth (*Harré* 1986; Moon 2008). 'Feelings', like other types of responses, are complex constructions, and do not have some special status as 'truth' that protects them from interrogation. This view enables us to expand our questioning of ourselves, and be more aware of the effort required to understand the responses of those from other cultures.

Our reactions to other people are rarely one-dimensional, which given the multiple nature of the self is unsurprising. However the language that we have available may suggest a unitary response. The English language offers a vocabulary of distinct emotions, such as anger, rage, lust, love, fear, hatred and more, which in the hands of our great writers is capable of beautiful and powerful evocations of complex moods. In everyday conversational language, however, there is often an assumption that we feel one thing at a time, or that we ought to. We need to escape these strictures, and find ways of allowing ourselves to explore our contradictory and paradoxical experiences. Metaphor and poetry, for example, use language in which multiple layers of meanings and possibilities can exist simultaneously.

Responses then come in a variety of forms, often overlapping and paradoxical. Not only are our feelings complex and multidimensional, but they also challenge attempts to demarcate who exactly they 'belong to'. The popular distinction between 'my' feeling and 'your' feeling is problematic, for we know from our own experiences that emotions can be transmitted and shared, through literature, film, poetry and most powerfully, the presence of others.

Counselling and psychotherapy value this capacity that we have as humans to share experience, and use it as a way of building relationships and understanding other perspectives. Here in particular, it is necessary to be aware of the co-constructed nature of emotion and the significant contributions that both client *and* therapist bring to their interactions.

The western concept of the independent, separate and autonomous individual is challenged by this complex shared experience. If we are all separate individuals, then it must be possible to define who owns which feeling, and to explain the way in which emotion appears to be able to move from person to person. Perhaps the most familiar explanations come from psychodynamic theories, with concepts such as projection, introjection, identification and projective identification. All of these involve the attribution or transmission of emotion from one body to another without conscious awareness.

'I know you're annoyed, I can tell by the way you look!' said Sarah. Bernice was indignant. 'Don't tell me how I feel! I'm perfectly happy – it's you that's cross, not me.'

One classic explanation would involve Sarah 'projecting' her feelings of annoyance onto Bernice. Another would suggest that Bernice projects **her** annoyance onto Sarah, and then disowns it. These types of concepts offer an account of relationships that relies upon processes analogous to sending invisible parcels of emotion to each other, which are accepted or rejected to varying degrees. Projective identification takes this one step further, in positing an unconscious transfer, which then is accepted and acted upon, all out of awareness. Definitions of these processes change through time and they are generally no longer seen as one person (usually the client) 'dumping' unconscious material upon the other (the therapist). Rather they are recognized as complex exchanges that occur between people who are both instrumental in their creation and maintenance. Transference and counter-transference are perhaps the most generally used of these types of ideas in counselling and psychotherapy, and they too need to be understood as co-constructed interactions.

There are studies in neuropsychology that demonstrate the existence of a mirroring activity in brain function (Gallese 2003, 2009). When I watch someone accidentally trap a hand in a door, the patterns that fire off in my brain mirror those of that person. A similar pattern is fired off if I see an image of someone's hand being trapped in a door, or if my own hand is trapped. The difference between my pain, your pain and the imagined pain is one of intensity in the discharge of the mirror neurons. Gallese terms this 'embodied simulation', a process that generates information that enables us to understand both the action and the emotion of others. It is suggested that this process underlies the development of empathy. The thing that we call our 'own' experience is never completely separate from the experience of those to whom we are relating, or are in the presence of, because as humans we are always unconsciously scanning the other.

The maps or neural pathways that we construct through experience and repetition guide us through life. New pathways can build upon old, sharing some characteristics and developing others. This constant activity of appraising, mapping, mirroring and patterning takes place in various parts of the brain without any conscious awareness. We are transmitting and decoding signals constantly. It has been suggested that the unconscious communication thought to underlie projective identification, for example, arises from subtle physical cues such as posture, facial expression, tone, breathing etc. that are processed and responded to out of awareness (Meissner 2009). Many of the ways in which we appear to transmit emotions and attitudes to each other can be thought of in terms of this type of activity.

We appraise a situation using the maps and mirrors that we already have, fit it into a recognizable pattern and respond accordingly. In order not to be overwhelmed by information, we need to condense and simplify it. A situation may be a highly complex, multi- dimensional mix of physical activity, spatial configurations, sound, language, visual stimulus and emotional tone. There is too much information to attend to every detail and previous experience will sensitize us to particular recognizable features.

Resonance

This sensitivity can be thought of as a form of resonance. Certain frequencies or patterns can set up oscillations or vibrations, transmitting with varied strength and range. For example, there are particular musical instruments, such as the sitar, which have 'resonance' strings that are not themselves played but vibrate in sympathy with others. As humans, we are able to resonate with each other's experience and our physiological capacity to mirror brain activity can be seen as a key component. The ability to attune ourselves to the feelings of others, so vital in early development and crucial to the practice of psychotherapy, is a form of resonance.

One of the great advantages of thinking in terms of resonance rather than projective and introjective processes is its ability to capture processes of multiple rather than dyadic relationships. For this reason it is a familiar concept on group work (e.g., Brown 2006). We can resonate with complex patterns as well as discrete moments, capturing wide-angled emotional experiences. We can tune in to many parts of a drama rather than focusing on one character, so that in watching, experiencing or hearing about events we have multiple responses. We are also constantly predicting the next step, based on our experience of sequences. Somewhere in our brain functioning we are always one step ahead and this predictive disposition in itself can create resonances. We hear the beginnings of a story and map it in different ways according to our existing patterns. In this way, resonance is not just an echo or repetition, but itself generates new vibrations and patterns.

Context

Thinking about the nature of our responses to other people highlights the complex signals and cues that are exchanged and interpreted in every encounter. The meeting of client and therapist and the inter-relationship that may unfold needs to be understood in terms of these unconscious but explicable mutual resonances and dissonances. What also needs to be considered is the context.

Our responses are more than interpersonal. We are acutely aware not only of the other but the situation within which we encounter them, and this introduces other significant factors into the relationship. The physical environment may be perceived, for example, as containing or imprisoning and this will contribute to the process of relating. Psychodynamic practice, in particular, pays close attention to the physical space offered for therapy, recognizing that the relationship in the room is influenced by the room itself. Perhaps more influential than this, however, is the context of power, status and authority that the relationship is contained within. This has particular relevance not only for the client/therapist relationship, but the trainer/trainee and supervisor/supervisee relationships also. Whatever model is used, there is an inevitable power differential between a 'helper' and a 'helpee'. There are ways to minimize this, but as long as there is a distinction between client and therapist roles, this power imbalance is always present (Proctor 2002).

First impressions

Meeting someone for the first time involves a mutual appraisal operating at different levels of awareness. We have already started to think about the nature of our responses and the context within which they are taking place and have identified some of the key categories we use to locate the other in our social world. We are scanning first of all for friend or foe, and if there seems no significant threat we then try to make sense of the other by positioning them according to markers that characterize our society. With scant information, we can still have a powerful response, as this exercise demonstrates.

Points for reflection

Choose two people from this list. You will be in the sole company of these other two people for a day. You have no information about why you are together or what you are doing but still need to make a choice between:

1. Male, white, 60s
2. Female, black, 40s, disabled
3. Female, 20s, white, lesbian
4. Male, 50s, working class, white
5. White female, 70s
6. Upper class female 40s
7. Middle class, Asian, male, 30s, gay
8. White 30s, with a clearly masculine physique but dressed in women's clothes.

Even with this minimal and crude information, we will have preferences. The point is not to expose any underlying prejudice in order to criticize or humiliate, but to notice and question our own responses. Trying to catch sight of and acknowledge these foundational attitudes and perceptions is an ongoing, challenging but essential task in personal development (Lago and Smith 2010).

Gender is unavoidably at the heart of who we are, how we respond to others and how they react to us. How we think about gender, how we understand it and how we live it will form a major part of any exploration of self. What does it mean to be a 'man' or a 'woman'? Why are there only two categories when we arrive in the world with a range of genital and chromosomal variations? Why pay so much attention to these particular features?

The moment we engage with these questions, we encounter stereotypes. These are powerful influences, whether or not we conform or rebel. Do we believe that men are less capable of expressing their emotions than women? We used to believe that women were incapable of driving cars or managing money. Enduring truths about each gender have revealed themselves to be social and historical constructions. Is there anything 'essential' that we can use to define male and female? Or do we need to think about masculinities and femininities in the plural, as available cultural expressions of identity (Maguire 2004)?

Gender stereotypes come entwined with **sexuality**. Those that apply in the heterosexual frame can be overturned in the homosexual. Gay culture subverts and challenges what the heterosexual group claims to be the proper order of things. There are stereotypes here too, of a different construction, but also limiting and unrepresentative of what for many is their lived experience of being lesbian, gay or bisexual. Different sexual identities and practices may challenge, stimulate or disturb; your response is an important ingredient in becoming aware of yourself (Moon 2008).

From the global to the local, there is nowhere unaffected by the powerful emotions that **racial** and **ethnic** difference generates. In many parts of the world, ethnic identity is more crucial than national identity so that, for example, being Welsh is more salient than British or Kurdish than Iranian. The ethnic group that gives us our identity generates a fierce emotional allegiance whenever it is threatened, and the world is full of violent conflicts that demonstrate this.

Attitudes and emotions surrounding racial and ethnic difference are profoundly ingrained, and like all our basic foundational attitudes, they are resistant to change. Few people are comfortable with an image of themselves as racists and many like to feel that it is an issue that they have already 'dealt with'. However, in the context of developing self awareness, it is always important to challenge any assumption that there is nothing more to be said, and particularly so in this area (Lago 2006).

Despite sporadic media reports that it is no longer significant, **social class** remains a highly significant means of distinguishing them from us. It is a key indicator of health, education, mobility and economic status. Every society makes fine discriminations between people and orders them into a hierarchy of importance and power. As a member of that society we are able to recognize these distinctions unthinkingly, in a way not possible for the non-member. In turn, we fail to recognize the status markers in other communities, assuming a far less complex structure than the 'insider' could reveal (Kearney 1996; Balmforth 2009).

Some readers may be surprised by the suggestion that **age** might influence their choice. Those who have experienced the subtleties of age discrimination will know otherwise. Status, authority, respect, economic power, physical well-being and sexual desire are often bound together with age in western society. We might avoid the elderly because old people are irritating, or seek them out because they are not threatening. They may represent comforting grandparents or dependent children, but they are unlikely to represent powerful high-status authority. Neither do the young. There are stereotypes for each age group that we draw upon in the absence of personal knowledge as we make our choices (Bytheway 2010).

Disability presents us with yet another category to inhabit or to respond to. Like sexuality, it is not necessarily visible, but it can disturb and disrupt us. It challenges our definitions of 'normal' and 'natural' and has the power to control relationships and social interactions. It can confront us with our physical limitations, vulnerabilities and mortality (Wilson 2003).

Having separated out these various strands, we need to put them back together. We always belong to more than one of these major categories or groupings and in reality it is impossible to separate out these dimensions of our group memberships. Gender, sexuality, class, race, ethnicity, age and ability, all intersect and interact to create a complex position.

Difference and similarity

We are more likely to be comfortable with those whose self has been created in a similar context as our own. We 'know' about these people in an unquestioning way because in so many regards they are us and we are them. We can take for granted a high level of mutual recognition: indeed at times we may take too much for granted, assuming that we are alike in every way. The bedrock of similarity can provide the security to explore and to risk intimacy. This does not mean that in all respects we have to be similar, but we need enough 'like me' ingredients to be able to embrace the 'unlike me' aspects in any relationship. Then these differences can provide the stimulation, excitement and vitality that we need and that security alone lacks. When we encounter people who are different from us, we can respond with interest, curiosity and an eagerness to learn from their other perspective. This generally works well as long as we do not feel threatened by their difference. If it appears that this different sort of person may take control, hurt us or confront us with some problematic areas of ourselves, then we move from curiosity to self protection.

Groups

A useful way of thinking about this concerns group membership. Whether we like it or not, we are group creatures. We are born into groups and live our lives within groups – family, friends, school, work, sports, church and hobbies as well as the wider groups of gender, ethnicity, social class and culture. People who are similar to us are members of the same groups that we ourselves belong to, and the common experiences create a level of understanding and security that we need in order to relate at any depth. That does not make us identical for we belong to many varied groups and have to find our own path through the conflicting influences and pressures that they bring. Our unique identity derives from the ongoing, complex negotiations between competing demands and responsibilities of these multiple group memberships.

Despite cultural assertions of individuality and independence, we have no existence outside of this group context. We are programmed to relate from birth, because exclusion from the group is life threatening. The first two decades of most people's lives are not dominated by one-to-one relationships but by group experiences of different kinds. Our clients come with feelings of depression, isolation and anxiety, for example, but our conversations will probably turn to their difficulties and problems in relating to members of their family group, peer group, work group, social group and so forth. Even though we might try to focus exclusively upon their internal world, we find that it is only comprehensible in relation to experiences in the social world. Finding out more about ourselves will take us along a similar pathway.

Points for reflection

You might like to reflect upon the groups that you belong to at this point in your life. Remember the larger groupings such as gender, social class and ethnicity as well as those such as family, religion, occupation, sports teams, college, hobbies, neighbourhoods and so on.

Can you recognize a characteristic part or parts that you play within groups?

What are the groups that you feel comfortable in? What makes them comfortable – size, membership, duration, activity or something quite different?

Are there times when membership of one group comes into conflict with that of another?

This avenue for self exploration can provide fertile ground for personal development, and to illustrate this I want to introduce you to Alison, a fictitious trainee counsellor on placement in a student counselling service at a large inner city college. At first sight she and her client, Owen, appear to share membership of the same racial and cultural group but differ in terms of age and gender, while social class is unclear. Is this significant?

Alison is white, middle aged, heterosexual and slightly overweight. She has been working for two months at the college, finding it both rewarding and difficult. The room she works in is cramped and stuffy, cluttered with other people's books and files.

Owen is 20, white, apparently heterosexual and looking physically very fit. He is a large presence in this small room. He has come to counselling on his tutor's recommendation, after breaking up with his girlfriend Kelly and binge drinking. He and Alison have agreed to work together for six sessions and then review.

They have met on three occasions, and Alison finds herself not looking forward to their next session even though it all seems to be going well. Owen seems open and quite happy to talk about himself, Kelly, his family, his hobbies, his mates and his drinking. He tells Alison that he finds the sessions really helpful – so why does she feel a wave of 'something' when she sees his name in her diary?

What is the something? She decides that she needs to try harder, to listen more carefully in the next session and to 'really empathize'. At the end of the fourth session, however, she is able to recognize that trying harder to be the good counsellor has not changed her feelings. In fact, listening to him talk about how unreasonably his ex-partner behaved, it was hard not to sympathize with the girl friend. Alison realizes that she needs to understand much more about her own reactions before they meet again. She decides to talk about him in her supervision group, but one of the other supervisees is having a crisis and there is no time left to discuss Owen.

Alison then decides to explore this on her own by writing down as honestly as she can what it is that she feels when she is with Owen.

Alison feels quite embarrassed or even ashamed of some of her feelings, but knowing that they can be valuable encourages her. When she thinks about her first impressions, Alison remembers feeling slightly alarmed by the physicality of this young man. Once they began to talk, however, this seemed to evaporate, and Alison found him friendly and cooperative. Then he began to appear as quite attractive, although Alison was quick to tell herself that he was young enough to be her son.

Now he seems far from attractive: She wants to get away from him, if she is honest. Those first impressions have receded into the background making way for the next stage in which the relationship begins to develop a degree of familiarity. Owen and Alison are beginning to feel that they know what to expect when they encounter each other, and the scene is set to explore exactly that – the familiar. This is the process that we go through in all our relating, moving through strangeness to familiarity. We use our existing maps of relationships, creating together familiar patterns, cuing and signalling each other in ways that we do not see. We end up in familiar dramas that are very often family dramas, for part of the structure of ourselves comes from the family group.

But Alison has not reached that point just yet in her understanding. She is still thinking about why she does not want to be in the room with Owen. She feels irritated, maybe even angry with him, and once she has given herself permission to feel this, starts to write down all the things that annoy her about him. He never shuts up, going on and on, all about himself as if he is the centre of the universe. He nods when Alison says anything, but then just carries on from where he left off talking about himself. He rarely looks at her directly, but focuses his gaze just above her forehead. 'It's as if he's talking to some animal perched on the top of my head!' she writes crossly.

Then she feels a wave of compassion for the young man who on the one hand seems full of his self importance, and on the other is struggling with his relationships. Alison approves of this response in herself, but she is smart enough to recognize that it may have diverted her from more negative feelings. She finds it difficult to explain, but feels somehow intimidated by him. It is not that she is frightened of him, of course –- or is it?

There is already enough material here for Alison to see that some of her feelings are familiar and to look at the resonances that are emerging. Her own father was loud and frightening, and her brothers took delight in bullying her. She was never able to fight back effectively. Suddenly Alison understands her empathy for the girl friend; she thinks that she has far more in common with Kelly than with Owen. How is this useful when Owen is her client, not Kelly?

Difference now plays its part, and on this occasion it is gender that needs thinking about. The power imbalance between men and women in society is part of the social world that has shaped both Alison and Owen and is present in their encounter even though not necessarily recognized. This underlying division has also found expression and been heightened by Alison's particular experiences of men. She has mapped onto a familiar scenario in her own experience, of male domination and physical bullying. This is valuable information both in terms of her own self exploration and development, and of her client's experiences. If this bullying scenario has emerged as she and Owen get to know each other, then it is highly relevant for both of them. If she is intimidated in the room, perhaps this is part of Owen's experience also. They are both caught up in a drama; Alison might give Owen the role of male oppressor, but it is quite possible that Owen feels himself to be oppressed. He is physically confined in a small space with someone who in his eyes has more power than he does. Perhaps that is why it is safer not to meet her gaze.

Owen came to counselling because of a problem in his relationship with a woman. If Alison is now thinking about gender then it is not unreasonable to wonder about Owen's underlying attitudes too, and the impact they might have had in his relationship with Kelly. Much of his behaviour supports a stereotypical version of masculinity, but perhaps part of him is struggling with questions about what it is to be a man or what sort of man he might become. When Alison thinks back through some of the sessions she can see points at which this conversation might have developed if she had intervened.

It is enormously helpful in terms of the counselling to be able to identify the 'bullying' scenario. The personal work for Alison is to recognize the ways in which she might be contributing to it, and to alter her behaviour enough to prevent it from being maintained over any length of time. Exploring her own passivity and sense of helplessness, for example, could put her in touch with other more assertive and interactive aspects of herself. Very subtle shifts in the person of the counsellor can have a significant impact upon what happens in the counselling room. If Alison can react differently to Owen, then he stands a chance of responding differently to her. It may well be that they find themselves talking about bullying, for example, with Alison discovering that Owen knows something of this, and it might also open up a conversation around masculinity.

Getting familiar

The story of Owen and Alison takes us from first impressions into the regions of familiarity. We all bring into our relationship the patterns that we have from previous life experiences, resonating with each other and drawing out particular configurations that jointly recreate something deeply familiar. Like dancers, we discover how to move together, each inviting or subtly directing the other to perform the routines we do well.

Alison needs to understand her own dance routines; that is, her contributions to the performance in the room. These are not easily deciphered and not readily let go of, for we all hold very tightly to the ways that we have developed to preserve the familiarity of our inter-personal and intrapsychic worlds. The things that we believe about ourselves need to be maintained to give us security, and we recruit oth-ers to support our versions of ourselves. To use another metaphor, it is as if we have a number of well-rehearsed dramas that we need to find actors to perform. For example, there is a drama called 'I am too needy' that requires a character who begins by being wonderfully supportive, then becomes exhausted and finally rejecting, proving once again that the 'I am too needy' is not just a story but *real*. The ideal person to play this role is one with a drama called 'I give and give but people just take advantage of me'. The many and subtle ways in which this scenario is co-created are generally ignored, but within a therapeutic relationship they can be identified and challenged.

The client in this is supported by the therapist. The therapist needs to find herself an arena within which she too can be challenged and supported to recognize her own dramas. Alison has made a good start, using her own resources, but needs more to take it further. The foun-dational assumption of psychotherapy and counselling is that talking with others is a powerful medium for self exploration and change. Engaging in dialogue with particular others could help her to extend the learning, and the next chapter goes on to look at learning from conversations.

Further resources

Kearney, A. (1996). *Counselling, Class and Politics*. Ross on Wye: PCCS Books.
Krause I. (1998*). Therapy Across Culture*. London: Sage.
Lago, C. (2006). *Race, Culture and Counselling: The Ongoing Challenge*. 2nd edition, Milton Keynes: OU Press.
Lago, C. and Smith, B. (Eds). (2010). *Anti-Discriminatory Practice in Counselling and Psychotherapy*. 2nd edition. London: Sage.
Maguire, M. (2004). *Men, Women, Passion and Power: Gender Issues in Psychotherapy*. Hove: Routledge.
Rose, C. (2008). *The Personal Development Group: The Students' Guide*. London: Karnac.
Wilson, S. (2003). *Disability, Counselling and Psychotherapy*. Hampshire and New York: Palgrave Macmillan.
Woodward, K. (ed.) (2004). *Questioning Identity: Gender, Class, Ethnicity*. 2nd edi-tion. London and New York: Routledge.

Fiction is a great resource in exploring relationships. Tastes vary but these are a few suggested authors to read for their treatment of contemporary relationships: Salley Vickers, Ian McEwan, Patrick Gale, Lionel Shriver and David Lodge.

Christopher Bollas, Michael Eigen and Irvin Yalom write in different styles about relationships in the context of therapy.

4
Developing through Conversations

Chris Rose

We have conversations in all areas with all sorts of people and many of these are enormously valuable in helping us to see ourselves from different angles. Talking with others is the fundamental activity of counselling and psychotherapy and this has to play a leading role in developing self awareness. I want to focus initially on the particular conversations that counsellors and psychotherapists might experience as part of the training context, such as personal therapy, supervision and the personal development (PD) group. These offer different styles of conversations that have the potential to teach us more of who we are and can, most importantly, enable us to have different sorts of conversations with ourselves.

The people that we meet and the relationships that we develop in these settings are in many ways no different from any other. They are coloured by difference and similarity, by our varied group memberships and associated power and by the contexts. They are co-created using the patterns and behaviours learnt through life. However, the particular context of training brings its own challenges and benefits that are likely to have a significant impact upon these relationships.

Power and authority

Perhaps the greatest challenge comes from issues of power and authority. Power is a tricky subject and always needs qualifying – over whom, in what respect, on what basis and in what circumstances are good questions to ask. Here I am using it as 'power to influence the outcome of training'.

From the previous chapter, it is clear that certain trainees arrive with more power than others, in that they are members of those groups that in our society can make things happen. Perhaps they come with more confidence and expectations of success than those from groups who are marginalized and need to constantly struggle to make themselves visible in society. Configurations of power that the training group brings to the course will be met by the power structures of the course itself. Course staff and supervisors have the legitimate power, or authority, to influence who passes and who fails the course. In the adult world, we know that we will be judged and assessed and we consent to this happening.

If the boundaries of confidentiality are clear, and trainees know which conversations will be shared, who with and for what purpose, then all of this can be accommodated. That does not mean that it has no impact, of course. Few of us have uncomplicated attitudes to authority, or arrive on a training course without years of experience of authority in educational institutions. Because we are multiple selves it is perfectly possible to accept the requirement of personal therapy, for example, and to also feel deeply resentful about having no choice.

All of us at various stages in our lives are told what to do and given no choice. As part of living in society we need to conform to rules and norms of behaviour, and we accept certain constraints as legitimate. In childhood, parents, care-givers and teachers dictate what is and is not acceptable; our reactions to these early authority figures play a part in our adult responses to managers, bosses, therapists, tutors, supervisors and the law in general.

Points for reflection

Think about authority in your own family of origin. As a child, who did you see as the most powerful person, and over what? Was power shared or in the hands of one person? Was there a hierarchy of power?

How would you describe your characteristic responses? Were you compliant, openly rebellious, quietly resistant, subversive or manipulative, for example?

What was your attitude to authority at school? Was this influenced by your peer group? Did it change at adolescence? Did you have what you consider to be good experience of authority?

How would you describe your attitude to authority at work? Have there been conflicts with managers or supervisors?

What is your experience of being in authority over others? Are you comfortable with this? Are there particular situations that you find difficult? What is your style of management?

A better understanding of our reactions to and perceptions of authority enables us to engage more flexibly with the person who embodies these attributes. Ideally we can discuss these issues with them, but this is not always possible. Therapists, supervisors, trainers and group facilitators are not perfect models. Like trainees, they vary enormously in their abilities and aptitudes, with different styles of relating, different ideas about their role and with strengths and weaknesses just like the rest of the human race. All we can assume is that they are more knowledgeable and experienced in certain areas than the trainee, and that, like the trainee, they are doing the best they can. I would like to think as well that they are actively engaged in the process of developing their own self awareness. Acknowledging power differentials does not have to involve either idealization or denigration, but needs to be worked with if the relationship is to achieve a more equal and balanced profile. If for some reason this cannot be part of the conversation in the room, then it needs paying attention to in other ways rather than resignation or resentment.

Time

If issues of authority present one of the significant challenges for conversations in training, then time offers a considerable benefit. Conversations in the three areas, therapy, supervision and PD group, continue from meeting to meeting over a substantial period of time. It is one of their strengths that material can be talked about again and again, from different perspectives, over the course of the relationship. When themes or difficulties arise, there is the opportunity to understand and work with the process as well as the content, rather than avoid or deny it. Understanding is gained through a process of linking and connecting experiences, thoughts, associations, felt-senses and physical sensations in such a way that a comprehensible and believable narrative can emerge. These webs of connections join the therapist to the client, the client and the therapist to their own interpersonal environments, the supervisor to the supervisee, colleagues to colleagues, trainees to trainees and so forth. Through these interconnections it becomes possible to make sense of interactions in which we are not physically present, and they are a key ingredient in supervision, enabling a supervisor to get a sense of what is happening between client and trainee therapist. This is usually referred to as 'parallel processes' in which relational patterns are mirrored in different areas, making it possible to understand 'from outside' what might be happening 'inside' the counselling relationship. This is a type of resonance, mapping onto patterns and configurations in the other. It is far more extensive than the word 'parallel' implies, involving a range of resonances that ripple like sound waves across wide territories, being picked up, deciphered and broadcast again by our internal transmitters.

Alison

I want to illustrate this by continuing Alison's story of growing self awareness as she explores her experience with her client in the three settings of personal therapy, supervision and the PD group.

1. Personal therapy

Alison chose Robert as her therapist because he seemed a gentle and thoughtful man with whom on first meeting she felt comfortable. This is how Robert describes Alison to his own supervisor.

She smiles a lot and is generally very quiet, apart from asking questions. She asks for my opinion and ideas often, as if I am some sort of guru, and I find myself talking far more than I would normally do. I can feel myself as quite inflated somehow – puffed up by her interest and attention. When I catch hold of this and get back to my usual self, there is little conversation. We sit in silence until Alison introduces another topic that she is interested in and wants to know my opinion of. Then I can feel myself getting irritated, as if there is no other conversation possible, apart from this teacher-pupil one. There's no one else to interact with in the room.

But just last session, she told me about being bullied by her brothers, thinking it might be affecting her counselling work. So I think I am just beginning to understand what is happening to us together in the room – why she shrinks herself into such a small placatory space and I become inflated. I'd like to explore this with her when we meet next.

When this exploration takes place it will hopefully enable Alison to see more of how she is contributing to a familiar pattern, and enlarge her understanding both of past and present. There are more parallels that emerge in her supervision group also.

2. Supervision

The following week, Alison does find some space in her supervision group to talk about Owen and her negative feelings. She explains that she couldn't talk about it in the last session because Nicky seemed to need the space far more.

The supervisor reminded her that she had been asked at the beginning of the session whether she had anything important to bring, and she had said not. 'It wasn't as important as Nicky's business,' she says.

Nicky then says that she feels bad about taking up all the time, and wishes Alison had said something. James joins in expressing his annoyance that Alison had said nothing. The supervisor comments on the link between both Owen and Nicky taking up all the space without any intervention from Alison. Now Alison is feeling upset that the other members of the supervision group are irritated with her, and she is finding it hard to concentrate.

Alison also has one-to-one supervision on her placement, and picks up the themes there when she has had a chance to think further.

She talks about being upset in the supervision group, because the last thing she wanted to do was annoy the others. Her placement supervisor asks her what is so awful about annoying people. 'That's how you get bullied, of course, by being annoying,' Alison responds. 'So you must tiptoe about and never upset anyone?' They go on to talk about Alison's own annoyance with Owen and in the course of the conversation 'annoyance' becomes 'anger'. Alison struggles with the image of herself as angry, but can acknowledge that it might be right. Her supervisor suggests that there may be some important issues for Alison around anger, particularly her own, that she might like to explore in her therapy.

The next stage in the learning conversation takes place in the PD group.

3. PD group

Nicky talks about her experience in the supervision group, saying that she felt terrible. She felt that Alison was indirectly accusing her of being greedy, taking up so much time, but wouldn't come out with it and say it directly. 'It made me look needy and demanding, and that's not fair!' says Nicky.

James says that it had irritated him, and then someone else links it to Alison's reticence in the PD group to take up any space. 'You only say anything if we ask you, and then you pass it on quickly to someone else.' Other group members join in and a discussion develops about 'trying to be invisible' and how it is impossible to get close to someone who never takes any risks in the group. Some members are sympathetic, wanting to know how they can help Alison say more; others are irritated, seeing her as ducking out of the work of the group and keeping herself safe.

The facilitator then wonders whether Alison might feel picked on here, and asks if Alison is really the only person in the group who finds it difficult to take risks.

In all of these areas, the conversations are teasing out more strands of a story. One strand is working with images and ideas of space, inviting others to fill up space, to inflate and enlarge, keeping safe through taking no space and trying to be invisible. Another strand is working with irritation, and by giving that more space it enables it to grow into anger. Each conversation presents another slight shift of perspective, because the participants change and have their own resonances and associations to bring to the material. In addition each setting has different boundaries and agendas. In supervision the boundary that is set between discussing client material and personal issues may vary according to the style of the supervisor, the time available and other competing demands. In the PD group, the consensus may be that some personal issues are not appropriate and need to be taken elsewhere. The context itself shapes the available conversations.

Personal therapy offers the least restrictive context, but it is the least available or affordable for trainees, leaving supervision and the PD group to provide the facilitating conversation. Supervision is enormously influential here (Wheeler and Richards 2007; Folkes-Skinner, Elliot and Wheeler 2010) but it can be especially coloured by issues of authority and assessment that make it difficult to develop a good supervisory alliance. It also has as its prime focus the counselling work with clients. For many students the only dedicated space for their own personal development is the group of that name, which has variable success.

The personal development group

The PD group has enormous potential. Given that there can be no 'self' without 'other', and no 'individual' with 'group', it offers an environment that mirrors and demonstrates the complex web that binds us to others. We are born into groups and live our lives in groups. Trying to understand more about the 'self' is fundamentally a group exercise. At the same time, we often fear groups. We recognize their power to overwhelm, coerce, reject, hurt and humiliate because the group narrative of our lives has often been coloured by these sorts of experiences. The cultural valuing of autonomy and independence further encourages us to minimize our interdependence on others and treat groups as places to avoid.

Points for reflection

Becoming more aware of your fears and fantasies about groups is an important part of personal development. Look again at the exercise about group membership in the previous chapter and reflect upon your negative and positive experiences in groups. How have they affected your attitude about working in group settings?

There are two persistent phrases that are heard repeatedly about the PD group. One is that 'it is not safe' and the other is 'what are we supposed to do?' Both of these I have attempted to address in 'The Personal Development Group: The Student's Guide' (Rose 2008) and I would recommend that any trainee who wants more guidance to refer to this book. There is, however, a particular aspect of 'safety' that is helpful to examine here.

One of the most influential characteristics of a PD group is the overlapping membership with a teaching group. The people who share lectures, assignments, practical exercises, lunch and possibly social activities are also the people who sit next to each other in the group circle, where the agenda is to talk about themselves and each other in depth. In contrast, in a therapy group, the members meet for say, an hour and a half per week and that is the only legitimate contact that they have with each other. All of their relating apart from the fantasized elements is witnessed by other group members and is available for comment and analysis. The scope for forming subgroups and extra-group alliances is limited and any conflict is contained within the group setting. This offers a very different environment to that of the PD group in which anxieties about the consequences of speaking directly can seriously inhibit genuine communication. Any conflict in the group is feared to contaminate the whole college experience, with the potential for recreating childhood scenarios involving revenge, silencing, ganging up, subtle bullying, absences, complaints to staff and so forth.

This context, real or imagined, challenges the trainee in using the group to best advantage. However, accepting some limitations does not mean that useful work cannot be done and real insights achieved. For example, it is a fascinating environment in which to learn to listen. Every group member brings to the group those characteristic styles of communicating that they have learnt through immersion in their own unique environments. Looking miserable and saying 'I'm fine', for example, can mean any number of things, depending on the sender of the message and its intended recipients. In some families it is clearly understood as 'you've upset me and now I am withdrawing from contact'. There are many possibilities, and we will all translate it according to the language rules that we are familiar with. Conversations in the PD group involve us in a polyglot environment in which it is often a struggle to translate different ways of speaking and being. It is certainly confusing, but it is also good preparation for the close listening and decoding that is necessary in much client work.

Another strength of the PD group environment is its ability to demonstrate the impossibility of neatly distinguishing my feelings, responses and 'issues' from yours. It is a common occurrence for one group member to be describing an experience calmly while another member experiences the emotions that seem to belong to the story. Our ability to unconsciously communicate and resonate is revealed frequently in the group setting, proving rich material for learning about the self and other. Often this emerges in the form of conflict, creating for some a high level of anxiety. Indeed it is the possibility of conflict that for many makes the idea of a group most threatening. It is more likely for overt conflict to find a place in the PD group than in supervision or possibly personal therapy because of the issues of authority and assessment mentioned above. This makes it particularly valuable, albeit uncomfortable, for personal learning.

We have all learnt about conflict from our individual and collective experiences, and we have a range of responses and attitudes. The person who has been shaped in a context of aggressive physical conflict has very different responses than one who comes from an environment in which conflict is dealt with through passive withdrawal and silent disapproval. Different cultures also have their own style of anger, involving the ways in which it may be legitimately expressed and the meanings to be attached to behaviours.

Points for reflection

Here is an opportunity to reflect upon your own experiences.
  What did you learn about conflict in the family as a child? Was it openly or passively expressed, and were there particular people who expressed it?

> Was conflict seen as positive, negative or neutral? What was its characteristic outcome? Did it hang in the air for days, for example, or go underground until the next time? Could it be resolved?
>
> Was it acceptable for you to express anger? What are your memories of 'winning' and 'losing'?
>
> What were the acceptable styles of conflict for family members? Were there differences around gender, age, ability, status or other variables?
>
> (Rose 2008)

Understanding attitudes and responses to conflict are a vital ingredient in self awareness. Relationships that cannot survive conflict, disagreement and challenge are unlikely to be either close or creative. As counsellors or psychotherapists it is necessary to be able to tolerate and embrace a certain degree of conflict in order to build therapeutic relationships at any depth.

The divisions within society along the lines of class, race, gender and ability are always available as sources of conflict and can be the bedrock of many disputes. But shared memberships of all these foundational groups do not in themselves guarantee harmony, and it is useful to look further at what may generate conflict.

Kirstie and Donna just do not get on. Kirstie's tearfulness and helplessness have generated a very supportive response from many group members, but Donna is irritated by it, and not afraid to say so in the PD group. It is a conflict that is unresolved and that the group attempts to explain as 'a conflict of personality'.

Donna is confident, assertive and challenging. She is a single parent with one teenage daughter, and runs her own business. Kirstie appears quiet and anxious, married without children and working part time as a classroom assistant.

People we do not like or get on with may seem very different from us, but to see it as a 'conflict of personality' is to describe it rather than explain it. The contradictory 'attraction of opposites' thesis is another example of a description masquerading as an explanation. In the example above, with further information, it is possible to understand more.

Kirstie was the eldest of five children and all would agree that she was mother's favourite. The older Kirstie became, the more responsibility her mother gave her to look after the younger children until Kirstie was effectively parenting the whole family, including mother. It was as if Kirstie had to become mother herself in return for mother's devotion. Donna too came from a large family but she was the middle child of seven children. Here no one seemed to take a parental role and the children were largely left to get on as best they could. Donna's eldest sister had the warmest relationship with mother but she took no responsibility for her siblings in an environment marked by fierce rivalry and neglect.

Now it becomes possible to see that both women have shared experiences that resonate for each other. They unconsciously understand something of each other's early experiences of growing up with a lack of mothering despite the presence of mother. Perhaps in adult life they still are searching for a caring response, while holding tightly to the familiar knowledge that it will never happen or be enough. They have learnt to respond to the situation differently: Donna with a tough defensive stance and Kirstie with repeated appeals for help. But it is shared vulnerabilities that underlie the conflict, and this recognition can often unlock defensive and attacking positions.

If this conversation can take place, it might also reveal the involvement of other group members. Conflict in the group setting is always much more than a two-person incident and all members have a part to play. Sometimes one person may be unconsciously elected to express anger that is felt by a number of other members also. Who else was feeling irritated with Kirstie's behaviour but said nothing? Who else has experiences that resonate with Donna's and Kirstie's? What other tensions are not being addressed? Does this argument mask other conflicts that are more threatening? There are multiple resonances in any group and no single explanation is ever sufficient to capture the complexity of human relating.

Those with whom we come into open or covert conflict with have a great deal to teach us about ourselves. In many circumstances it is not possible for the people involved to explore together what lies beneath the surface, but a PD group can offer this environment. There are other valuable places where these sorts of conversations take place in the development of self awareness.

Conversations with our selves

We have the capacity to talk to ourselves, and this internal dialogue can provide a major impetus in expanding self awareness. Talking therapies rely upon dialogue to empathise, reframe, support and challenge. Through this it becomes possible for clients to look at themselves and others in a new light. We can offer ourselves those features of conversations that facilitate growth and development. Those areas that are most difficult to access will not reveal themselves in an instant, and our foundational attitudes only gradually become clearer as the conversation develops. If we can develop questioning ways of talking with ourselves that are curious rather than bullying we stand a much better chance of achieving this.

The self is not one dimensional and does not speak with one voice. We have a range of internal voices that become clearer as we start to listen more attentively. Initially it may only be possible to identify two or three, but this can swell into a more sizeable internal group that is enormously valuable in the development of self awareness. We are multiple selves so there is no reason to expect a two-person dialogue to dominate the internal conversations, but it is often the place to begin.

Alison, for example, began her enquiry into what was happening in her relationship with Owen by talking with/writing to herself. There have been significant conversations with others since then and now she is trying to understand more about her own anger. She imagines what might be helpful in understanding another person's anger and asks herself these questions. You might like to do the same.

Points for reflection

When is the last time you were openly angry? Does this happen often?

Did you feel comfortable afterwards or wish you had not said anything?

What sorts of things make you openly angry?

Who are the people that it is easy to be angry with, and who are difficult? Are there some people that it is hard to stand up to?

What outcome do you expect if you are openly angry? Where might this expectation come from?

Who were the angry people in your childhood and who are they now?

How do you show that you are angry if it is not spoken? Can you recognize this style in your own family?

The tone here is very important. This is not an interrogation but a curious search for information that also registers ways in which questions are responded to. What causes you to answer some rapidly without time to think, to avoid some or to feel annoyed, for example? This is an internal dialogue in which the voice asking the questions is fundamentally on your side, rather than an antagonist. It is a compassionate voice that has the capacity to challenge as well as support and reassure.

If Alison can find this voice within herself then it will be a valuable ally in her work ahead as a counsellor.

There are points in the dialogue when you might hear another voice. If responses such as 'I give myself a hard time' or 'I tell myself that it was OK' come up then there is another interesting question here. Who is giving who a hard time, or who is reassuring who? (I think it is hard to find a counsellor, psychotherapist or trainee who does not have an internal voice that criticizes their behaviour and attitudes.) Now there are at least three voices in this conversation and the group is beginning to form.

The internal group

Reflecting upon self and other through the medium of internal voices or characters is not a pathological activity but one that is widespread, if not universal. This is evidenced by the number of writers who have addressed this, in different ways: Mearns' 'configurations of self', Rowan's 'sub-personalities', Berne's parent/adult/child transactions, psychodynamic concepts of object relations and Jung's archetypes are some examples. The 'internal group' is a concept that draws upon these and other ideas in a style that it is hoped can be grasped and used in the development of self-awareness. It is used here as a metaphor – an imaginative way of engaging with one's selves and attending to the interactions between them.

Learning to listen to ourselves is part of learning to listen to others, and vice versa. Identifying the voices or characters that comment, direct, criticize, encourage and so forth is an interesting challenge. You may discover a Cinderella, a wicked witch, an Eeyore, a handsome prince, a nagging parent or a frightened child. Characters or voices are rarely simple representations of key people in our lives but rather composite mixtures taken both from our experience of others and from the powerful myths and stories that permeate the culture.

Points for reflection

Imagine you are asked to make a video that conveys the multiple aspects of yourself. Draw up a cast list of characters with varying ages. Who will have the starring roles and who will have the supporting ones? Are there 'good' and 'bad' characters? Do you have favourites?

The task of discriminating between the internal voices prompts careful listening. It is particularly valuable to be able to hear the mutterings of those characters who loiter around the edges of the group. These are often the key members who need to join the circle and contribute to the collective endeavour rather than attack or disrupt from the sidelines.

There are also likely to be voices that we do not want to listen to that the other more desirable characters try to silence. Any internal character that behaves in socially or morally unacceptable ways will always present problems. How do we deal with violence, sadism, destructiveness – the parts of ourselves and others that we fear? Should these characters be allowed into the group with the idea that they can be rehabilitated or that their power can be diminished? Or should they be locked away? It is a dilemma mirrored in the external world. There is no simple answer, but I would say that we need to develop the internal conversation rather than to close it down, recognising that all of us have unattractive, politically incorrect voices murmuring somewhere in the internal hubbub. The more we can hear them and respond to them internally, the less they will be able to covertly influence our relationships with others.

Having identified key characters it is then possible to look at how they communicate with each other. The styles are as varied as our own experience; they may shout, nag, sulk, panic, have tantrums, refuse to speak and so forth. Often they seem joined in partnership, so that, for example, 'Poor Me' triggers a response from 'Pull Yourself Together'. Our paradoxical and ambivalent attitudes can be represented in these pairings, but there are other alliances and subgroups operating also. How they communicate, how decisions are made and how power is distributed are all important factors in understanding ourselves.

In order to develop this awareness we need a part of the self that is observing and asking the questions. This character has the potential to take on the role of facilitating the group. The internal group faces many of the same challenges as a therapeutic group, needing some facilitative voice in order to draw out its creative rather than destructive potential and to help generate some new ways of relating. Dominating voices need to be moderated, silent members need to find a voice, members need to listen to each other and conflict needs to be managed and resolved. The character that grows into this role is also well prepared to act as internal supervisor and/or therapist.

At the same time as the internal group offers a way of reflecting upon ourselves, it helps in understanding the multiple self that is the other person. In a therapeutic relationship in which the therapist has reflected upon their own internal group, it becomes possible to identify the characters in the client's group. Resonances between client and therapist can be understood as members in each group talking to each other. For example, a therapist who has recognised and worked with their own internal disruptive adolescent is likely to clearly hear the adult/child confusion and rebelliousness in a client's story. The adolescent characters recognise each other, and there is an invitation to join forces, usually in opposition to some authority figure. Self-aware therapists are able to hear the invitation and consult their own internal group about how best to respond.

In the next chapter, Caroline Hall suggests a way of using the written word to access the voices and characters that populate the internal group. It is a metaphor that reappears at various points within the book as the focus moves to other means of communication. Conversations with ourselves and others can provide a valuable commentary upon other ways of communicating, and provide rich opportunities for personal growth.

Further resources

On groups

Behr, H. and Hearst, L. (2005). *Group-Analytic Psychotherapy: A Meeting of Minds.* London: Whurr Publishers.
Rose, C. (2008). *The Personal Development Group: The Students' Guide.* London: Karnac.
Yalom, I. (2005). *The Schopenhauer Cure: A Novel.* New York: Harper Collins.

On supervision

Henderson, P. (2009). *A Different Wisdom: Reflections on Supervision Practice.* London: Karnac.
Proctor, B. (2000). *Group Supervision: A Guide to Creative Practice.* London: Sage.
Shohet, R. (2008). *Passionate Supervision.* London: Jessica Kingsley.

On conversations with clients or patients

Eigen, M. (2005). *Emotional Storm.* Middletown: Wesleyan University Press.
Hobson, R.F. (1985). *Forms of Feeling: the heart of psychotherapy.* London: Tavistock Publications.

5
Developing through the Written Word

Caroline Hall

This chapter is about reading and writing as ways of knowing ourselves. A central concept in this book involves knowing ourselves through dialogue with other selves, and I want to explore in this chapter how we can do this from the interactions we have through written words – in reading and writing.

At this very moment, you have in your hands a special way of learning about yourself. You are reading words written by myself and others who all want to share our understanding of self knowledge and our ways of developing it. You also have at your fingertips a way of knowing yourself that is extraordinarily powerful. You have only to pick up a piece of paper and a pencil, or approach a keyboard, and write. With these two simple activities of reading and writing, you have access to the whole world of communication with other selves, including your own self.

As this book discusses, that world of communication we have with each other is the world in which we develop. From birth onwards, each one of us is immersed in a milieu of intricate and complex social relationships, interacting with other people in all kinds of ways – with our bodies, through spoken language, but also through the medium of written words. We read in the writing of others what they want to say to us, and we write what we want to say to them. These interactions using written words are like conversations but of a very special nature that is explored in the chapter.

Of all the dialogues that we might have with other selves, it is from the 'inner dialogues' with our own selves – those multiple parts of ourselves reflecting our development in a social world – that we can learn the most. In this chapter I want to show you how to conduct such dialogues using written words to make real those conversations and to learn from them. I know that some people will say with a hollow laugh 'I have only to pick up a pencil and write? Since when has that been ONLY? It's a terrifying thought'. So my task in this chapter is to show you how writing can become a friend who will listen to you carefully and who does not judge but will comfort and suggest things. I hope you will find that writing can be like being with a good therapist who says 'I'll be me and you are you', so you can fully meet the 'me' that you are.

Written words and why they are special

In the context of therapy and the subject matter of this book, words have a very special place. It is widely accepted that therapy of any kind works largely because of the relationship between the therapist and the client, but in the 'talking therapies', which include most forms of counselling and psychotherapy, the word is special. 'To put something into words' is often a crucial turning point for both client and therapist, when an experience becomes labelled and thereby transfigured. Words allow us to communicate about an experience and share it with other people, a social process that can normalise the experience. They somehow let us get outside of feelings and allow us to 'deal with' them better. The novelist Jeanette Winterson talks of words' ability to turn feeling into facts; in her own experience, literature 'gave pain a mouth' (Winterson 2009).

In the search to know ourselves better, words again have this same purpose, of expressing what we feel and linking it to other people's experience. When words are then written – giving them a more tangible reality than that of sound waves – the process is carried further, and our inner experience is more fully realised. The word 'realize' itself is significant: something is made more 'real' when we see it written. The special effect of putting words on paper or computer screen is to give us a distance from the experience and thus, really to see it and more fully to know it.

Developing through reading

When we read, it is as if we are in conversation with another person. The vast stores of conversations represented in books, newspapers, journals, magazines and the internet give us access to countless other people who can tell us things about ourselves. There are different ways we can learn from them. First, as the chapter on thinking about the self discusses, we can learn about the self as a theoretical concept, from philosophers and psychologists. Linked to this is learning about the self from scientists who tell us how selves function – the biology of ourselves as living organisms and psychological accounts of the mind's mechanisms.

Another way of learning about ourselves is through reading material that allows us insights into other people's lives. Biography, of course, is a deliberate attempt to show us other lives, but other genres do this too. From history, we learn how people have lived in the past; from geography, anthropology and sociology we learn how people have lived and how they now live in other cultures and in other situations. Literature itself represents a vast source of knowledge of people's behaviour in the present, past and future in different cultures, in different circumstances and in different relationships. All the teeming, endless possibilities of human interaction are there when we read widely, and from this we have a context for our own experience.

Fiction is of special interest here. Keith Oatley, an experimental psychologist working on emotion, hypothesises that fiction works as a kind of 'simulation run' for understanding ourselves and others (Oatley 2008). Each of us in the single life we are allotted can only experience a tiny part of all possible things that human beings can be and do. In Oatley's view, through reading about people in other situations we get the chance to see what happens to them and we can learn from their experience vicariously.

Julian Barnes, the novelist, makes a similar point in a recent book. He remarks at one point that 'Fiction and life are different; with fiction; the writer does the hard work for us. Fictional characters are easier to see, given a competent novelist – and a competent reader. They are placed at a certain distance, moved this way and that, posed to catch the light, turned to reveal their depth'. It is this 'distance and depth' which I suggested above is the special characteristic of written words that allows us to learn about others and thus, about ourselves.

Fiction seems then to improve our judgements of what to do. Oatley quotes Gilbert, another psychologist, the author of *Stumbling on Happiness* (2006), who says people tend not to know themselves very well and as a result, often make poor choices about actions intended to bring happiness. Oatley has some experimental evidence that using fiction to learn about the self can improve how people respond in real life to emotional challenges. In similar ways, literature can be therapeutic in itself and useful within therapy (for more on this, see Liz Burns 2009). A kind of therapy involving the use of literature that is becoming increasingly widespread is known as 'bibliotherapy'. Until recently, this title just meant learning from self-help books, but it has come to mean much more. The author, Blake Morrison, has described the rise of a scheme called 'Get into Reading' as an 'experiment in healing, or less grandiosely an attempt to see whether reading can alleviate pain or mental distress' (Morrison 2008). He quotes from several authors and readers to show how literature can help. Reading, Morrison says, 'surreptitiously takes us inside ourselves, deeper than we might have expected or chosen to go', and borrowing the lovely phrase from Alan Bennett's 'The History Boys', describes how in the presence of great literature, 'it's as if a hand has reached out and taken our own.'

This experience of connection with another human being is perhaps the crucial thing in reading that helps us understand ourselves. Real life accounts may be even more powerful than fictional ones precisely because we know that another human being has really felt the same as us, and our own experience is affirmed.

What we choose to read is important. If reading is one side of a conversation, it is a rather special conversation that allows one person (the author) to hold the floor while we as readers have a choice about the level of engagement we have with the speaker. More easily than in spoken conversation, we can negotiate the interaction with the other person. We needn't even open a book, or we can skim it, read carefully and critique, shut it at any point, or throw it away if we don't want it. Choosing in these ways to whom we 'listen' makes it clear that reading – and learning from it – is not a passive process, and the choices we make are highly relevant to who we are. Even while writing this, pausing to look at my bookshelves, I am made aware of things about myself that although I knew, I did not fully realise. The particular books in this room are here as a result of a series of choices that I have made throughout my life, and now reading their titles and their arrangement, I am seeing myself reflected as if in a mirror.

You might like to try this exercise too, looking at the books you own or borrow, as if they belong to someone else. What is the person like who collects John Buchan novels, or who reads only Jane Austen? Why do they keep romance books in the bedroom? Why are there no books in the living room, and so on? Irvin Yalom, in writing about memories of someone who had died, quotes from a patient of his who had found it consoling to remember her mother's saying 'look for her among her friends'; I think we can also 'look for her among her books'.

Developing through our own writing

1. The use of reflective writing

Learning from literature, then, allows us to discover how our experience of living compares with that of others, and may give us words with which to describe it. But of course, working as a therapist or counsellor, we have the enormous privilege of hearing directly about others' experience, and we have this day in and day out. I often thought that clients would learn more if they sat in my chair and simply had the experience of listening to other people who tell you in their thousand different ways that you are not alone in the world; that the fears and doubts, the pain and sorrows, that you know are shared by most humans.

Nevertheless, the understanding to be gained from this special experience is not given to us on a plate. We have to work to know our clients and why they are in trouble, and indeed, we have to know ourselves well to do that work. This kind of understanding is gained in various ways but a very important way is through writing used as an evaluative process or in so-called 'reflective writing'. This kind of writing, which essentially allows one to think in a reflective way, is widely used in many fields of professional training and practice. But in the field of therapy, a less common use, but in my view an even more valuable one, is to learn about yourself. If you are going to become a good therapist, the more you know about the self (you!) that is in interaction with the other who has come for help, the better. And regularly writing about one's work is a fantastic training for using the written word to learn about the self; indeed, it is such a valuable way of learning about the self that I am going to devote most of the rest of the chapter to it.

Julian Barnes says that in life, as opposed to fiction, 'the better you know someone, the less well you often see them. They may be so close as to be out of focus, and there is no operating novelist to dispel the blur.' He himself, in his book called *Nothing to be Frightened Of* (Barnes 2009), is using writing to help deal with his own fear of mortality and death. I want to suggest that in using reflective writing, we can all be our own 'operating novelist' (or playwright) to dispel the blur and see ourselves. In reflective writing, as the phrase suggests, we reflect on the subject of our Selves in writing, 'turning this way and that...to reveal the depth'. Writing gives us the distance that allows us to see more clearly and as I have described above, to *realize*. So how do we do it?

2. Developing the skill of writing reflectively

For some clues about developing this kind of writing, let us go back to the consulting room where, as I said, we daily meet other people and get to know them. We do this with a kind of gentle curiosity, listening very carefully to what they are trying to tell us, and receiving what we are told respectfully. Then later we write about what happened, allowing the experience fully to be absorbed, noticing our own thoughts and feelings and letting ideas come. It is this kind of approach that we need for getting to know ourselves.

   The first step is to develop fluidity in producing written words. A method of writing called 'free-writing' (Elbow 1973) can be very helpful here. It involves writing that simply receives the words forming in your brain without the intervention of an 'internal editor' who might criticise or reject what is said. Gillie Bolton, who has also written widely on using this kind of writing (see, for example, Bolton 1999), calls it 'writing from the end of the pencil'. We might see this as getting away from too much conscious thought and letting the unconscious speak instead.

Points for reflection

Free writing

The basic principle of free-writing is that once you start writing, you must keep your pen (or pencil or fingers on the keyboard) moving and producing words whatever the sense or grammatical mistakes. Nothing matters except producing words.

   As a warm-up, get ready to write wherever you feel comfortable and without distraction. You're going to write for 30 seconds only so look round the room, pick an object and using that as your starting point, write. You might need a stopwatch to help you. *You must keep writing without stopping until time is up.* If you get stuck, write 'I'm stuck, don't know what I'm doing' or whatever swear words or panic words come to mind – it does not matter!

   Then do the same, but write for one minute.

   Now you're ready to write for five minutes. You might start at one point but finish with another. The idea is simply to practise writing freely. It's worth repeating that if you get stuck, just write that you're stuck. However bad this feels, you *will* find that words come.

   The next step is to practise writing while 'turning (your object) this way and that'. You can even try holding an object in your hand and turning it round, feeling its weight, really observing it through your experience of holding it, and writing directly from that experience.

You should find that words flow more comfortably through practice, but as well as freeing your words, you are also developing an attitude of gently noticing or 'mindfulness', and this is so important in getting to know yourself.

The next step is to use your writing to learn about yourself. For this, you will write about something in yourself that you have been noticing, something that needs attention or something about you that you want to know better. Finding this starting point is a skill in itself, and may need practice as suggested below.

Points for reflection

Finding a starting point to write

Set aside time to write, and then in the period leading up to it, gently mull over what you might like to write about, allowing thoughts to surface.

Any subject is worth writing about to begin with. It won't be just random, but it will have some significance, and you can even reflect on why a particular topic has come to the surface.

Start noticing the 'clouds' in your mind, so to speak, the things that are overshadowing you. It might be a sense of anxiety about a forthcoming occasion, or a recent conversation. The cloud may only be the faintest wisp, a sense that not all is clear. It is this sense that we are trying to tune in to and amplify through writing.

Then start writing. You will probably find that the thoughts you have allowed and the feelings you have been mindful of determine what you write about. Turn them this way and that, and again, gently enquire 'I wonder what's going on here'.

For me, over many years of practice, it has become second nature to write in this way when I need to stop and discover what is happening in my life. I also believe that because each of us has to live with our self, we might as well get to know as much as we can about who that self is; but as I have already said it is also a vital part of becoming a therapist. The next section looks at how we can take these techniques and ideas further in learning about ourselves from the written word as fully as possible.

3. Using reflective writing to find your 'inner group'

In writing this chapter, I had to experiment with several voices that I might have used – all of them mine but each would speak differently to you. I chose one as the most suitable but as I write, I am aware most of the time of other voices that want to say things. For example, there is a voice that says 'What a load of rubbish!' there is one that says 'Haven't you finished yet? I want to go outside'; there is another that wants to talk about the psychology of communication and the concept of 'words'; there is the voice of my playful self who keeps tugging my sleeve and wanting to make jokes, and so on. These several voices are an example of what earlier chapters imply in discussion of the self as being socially determined, and consisting of multiple selves.

Of course, in writing this chapter, my other voices have had to keep quiet because the format of a book chapter normally requires what is essentially a monologue. Yes, I am in conversation with you as the reader, but in a particular role only; my other selves would be inappropriate here. And similarly, in most discussions of reflective writing as a method of development of self awareness, only one self is expected and only one voice is heard. But if the self is actually made up of several voices, we risk getting a very one-sided view of that self in this process. It would be like being in a room full of people but talking only to those who are known or only those who push themselves forward. The quieter ones or the unknown ones, or the ones who say uncomfortable things, these are ignored.

So how can we become aware of these other voices and learn about ourselves as fully as this book promises? What we need to do is start exploring what other voices might be there; like me while writing this, you may already be aware of one or two others that seem to take part in conversations in your head. Getting to know them is the next step, a process very much like getting to know another person in the external world: finding out their names, letting them talk, and, crucially, listening to what they have to say.

At this point, we must deal with the matter of 'hearing voices' with respect to the diagnostic characteristic of schizophrenia. There is much debate about the provenance of 'voices' in schizophrenia, and indeed about the unity of any such condition. My own position is that, as this book repeatedly argues, most people actually experience some kind of dialogue inside their heads. We talk to ourselves and hear different responses, but when someone begins to hear the voices as external to themselves, then something is amiss. For whatever reason, they are unable to own their voices, and the voices become externalised. In fact, one current way of helping people experiencing schizophrenic symptoms is actually to facilitate recognition and ownership of voices.

When I started to extend my own reflective writing, I began to try and capture conversations that were going on internally, writing them as fully as I could so that other voices were heard. I had already noticed that my reflective writing was becoming – literally – monotonous because there was always just one voice, a voice that I regarded as 'my voice', the 'true self' that I had been taught was there and that I had to discover. But as soon as I allowed other voices to be represented, this self became much more interesting, a rounder, fuller self. This idea has much in common with 'externalising' conversation, a practice used in narrative therapy (see, for example, Dale 2009), and with 'dialogical journal writing' (Wright 2009), two examples from a growing interest in writing as self-therapy.

A very effective development of these forms of writing reflectively that treats the self in this different, multifaceted way is to exploit the format of a play in which a cast of characters interact in conversation. By writing out the inner drama as a play, we have a way of realising the inner group of selves with their distinct voices. The notion of 'inner dialogue' becomes actual through its representation in writing. Through making the conversation appear on paper, we have the chance to listen to more of the voices in dialogue, to get to know more of the selves and understand something of their styles of interaction.

The following shows what this might look like. I have based it loosely on a recent dialogue within myself about writing this chapter. Using my own material in this way runs the risk of exposing things about myself that you may find ridiculous or embarrassing, but I want also to show that we can be open about ourselves with other people. Indeed, as I have indicated in the discussion of fiction, we need to hear from others what life is like for them and we will develop ourselves through recognition of our common bonds with other people.

HER INDOORS: OK guys! What about this job we've got to do?

ANXIOUS: My stomach is churning. I feel dreadful. We've bitten off more than we can chew.

PLAYFUL: Does it mean we'll have to stop having fun? I was really enjoying writing that pantomime with Doer.

SCEPTIC: It's all a waste of time anyway.

DOER: *This is really bad timing. I've got loads of other things I want to be doing, not only the panto, but all those gardening projects and the new choir.*

ORGANISER: *I wish you'd give me more time to sort out all these things you come up with.*

ALL: *It's all Her's fault! She got us into this.*

HER INDOORS: *But listen, everyone! You're such a good team. I think we can do this. Anxious, I do understand you feel bad, but I'd really like us to have a go. We'll look after you.*

ANXIOUS: *But have we actually got anything to say?*

SCEPTIC: *Probably not. It's just Playful having ideas again. Ideas are easy. It's the carrying them out that's the problem.*

PLAYFUL: *I wish you lot would be nicer to me! You all liked my idea!*

SCEPTIC (aside): *I didn't.*

HER INDOORS: *Sceptic, I sometimes wish you'd just go and boil your head – save your energy to spot real problems.*

DOER: *OK, we want to do this chapter, but I still want to go and do the other things.*

HER INDOORS: *Organiser, surely you can sort something out with Doer?*

PLAYFUL: *Now you're all going off to work and I'll be left alone. Who's going to play with me?*

HER INDOORS: *Oh, Playful, I'm sorry. You've been really helpful, but we can't play all the time. We've got to take things seriously now.*

PLAYFUL: *Ah, The Importance of Being Earnest?*

SCEPTIC: *Very funny.*

In this extract, several characters appear who speak in an orderly fashion. In reality, as I suggested above, an internal conversation is much less orderly, rather more of a babble of voices, some of whom might be discussing something sensibly, while others ignore them and carry on muttering about something else, while others sing or argue or poke fun. The extract shows how we can try to make sense of this noise, just as a play in a theatre has the task through accepted conventions, of representing real, disorderly conversations.

A question that immediately arises when working with the voices that are parts of ourselves is how do we know who they are? How shall we name them? You will probably find that you already recognise very well some of your inner selves and what you call them is a personal matter. It's your decision, your selves. In writing my own play, I had no difficulty in recognising Anxious, a voice who often speaks first particularly when faced with a challenge like writing a chapter! Another who is always around is Sceptic, who is a slightly depressing character but one who is often helpful in seeing both sides of a question. You may find you name your characters in quite different ways, just as we know other people by their nicknames, by their formal title or whatever.

In writing my play, very quickly a character emerged known as Her Indoors, who took a leading role, making arrangements to write, listening to and encouraging the other parts rather like a play's producer. The name 'Her Indoors' is slightly mocking but also jokey – maybe Sceptical and Playful thought of her name! She took the role like that of a group facilitator in an external group, who brings the group into existence and who helps the members work together in safety. As I have worked extensively with groups in the real world, and I have been a team leader in various settings, group facilitator felt a very natural role to include among the cast, and I could see many similarities between fostering an effective working group and facilitating my inner group. In particular, helping everyone to find their voice within a group seems to me to be of great importance, whether it is in a counselling service, a village committee or in my own head.

Other characters may take longer to be recognised. I have recently begun in my own dialogues to meet a character whose name I am still unsure of; this mirrors what happens in an actual group of people in which there will be some who prefer to remain silent while some hog the conversation. The virtue of using the play format to know oneself is that the quiet voices can be represented as part of the cast (just as they are actually present in a group, even if silent), and over time, they can be worked with to be understood and perhaps unblocked. In finding our unheard voices, we need to do the same things we have to do when we work with external groups such as encourage, listen carefully, make time for, reflect on why others are dominant and so on.

Unblocking unheard voices needs to be done with care and it may take a long time to achieve. There are many reasons why people do not contribute in a group; a very common reason is 'being shy'. Most people would say they are shy in groups and they find it hard to initiate interaction, but they can usually contribute when they feel safe. Silence may also be a protective device against conflict, or an expression of fears about what might be revealed in a group.

In our internal group, confidentiality is probably assured, but there are other reasons for fearing to be heard; if we hear about bad things, are we not bad people? Unleashing angry and hostile voices might disrupt a lifetime of carefully maintained equilibrium. But more positively, some voices may have been silenced by the dominance of others, and when we write our parts to read and know ourselves, we can hear those voices. Unblocking them is an enormously powerful experience.

Now that you have seen an extract of inner dialogue and with these comments in mind, you might like to experiment with writing your own dialogue. If you are a therapist or training to be one, you are probably already using the tool of self-reflective writing to develop your practice (and indeed, several professions now use this in their training, see Bolton 2001), so you could include this different format for self-discovery. After all, the best way to learn is through play!

The following points for reflection should help to get you started.

Points for reflection

Playwriting

Reflect on the selves that might make up the person that you know as your self.

Jot down some names or identifying labels for these selves.

Imagine you are entering a room where these characters are sitting.

Write for five minutes about how you feel entering the room. Who do you know well? Who would you like to get to know better? Is there anyone you dread speaking to?

Now write their imagined conversation in play format, first setting the scene and giving a short cast list.

Enjoy the writing! It's your play — you can direct the action, and write stage directions as you wish, but try letting the characters speak for themselves.

When you feel comfortable letting your known selves talk among themselves, set them a problem that you're dealing with in your outer world, e.g. an issue with a colleague at work that's causing friction. What do your selves think about it? What suggestions might they make about solving it?

Write their conversation as they try to address the problem.

Taking it further

Now we have written our selves as a cast of characters, we can get to know and understand them better. Like getting to know our friends, we need first to want to know them, and then to spend time with them. We need to see them in different circumstances, and let them speak about their experiences. A few minutes writing every day will give, over time, much material to learn from. A good starting point for doing this is to write about your interactions with other, real, people. So, for example, you might have met one friend for lunch, when you and she put the world to rights in a deep conversation; later in the day, you bump into another friend with whom you have a riotous few minutes, gossiping about the awfulness of people at your work. Here is meat for reflection, because in meeting two different people, you show a differing response to them, and we can say perhaps that the meetings engaged different sets of your inner selves. Writing subsequently about the difference in experience in terms of who met whom, will help to define the characters in your internal cast.

Another useful method is to start writing just by asking 'How is everyone today?' and see who wants to reply, and then check around with everyone else. The characters will become more familiar and you could try to learn more by encouraging them to talk about themselves and their history. You can even be quite directive and get different characters to kick off the discussion in turn; again, exploring the differences in response will help define and develop more of your inner voices.

Next you might try writing conversations between your characters in which they try and learn about each other, a process that mimics a group work session. Suppose, for example, that I want to know more about Playful, one of my inner group selves that we met earlier in this chapter. I could use the play format, getting the others in the cast to talk to her and ask her questions. I could also explore why she seems to be female whereas other characters seem more male – Sceptical, for instance. Playful seems also to be quite childlike so I might explore the links between her in my inner group and my experience as a child within my family, again by getting Playful to talk through the inner drama.

The role of the group facilitator – the character that I called Her Indoors – may need to be developed if you have not had experience working in this way with an external group. The key to the role is that the facilitator is able to create an environment in which people feel safe and that they are respected as themselves; in this atmosphere, each individual comes to play their part. A good facilitator does not need to lead all the time, but in learning the role at first, you may find that you want to intervene in all conversations. Gradually, with experience, you will be able to trust the members of your group to look after themselves and help each other.

Another step you might take in developing self-awareness is to explore relationships between the characters. There is much in even the brief extract above that provides us with some clues about these. What goes on between Playful and Sceptical, for example, looks to be a rich seam to explore. Again, we can use ideas about working with real groups to help us understand and explore the workings of our inner group, such as asking the group to look at why some members take a back seat in a group while others dominate. Thus, Playful and Sceptical might be invited to talk about their relationship by questioning what happens when Sceptical puts down Playful. How do they feel about each other? What do they want from each other? Another example from the illustrations concerns the self called Anxiety who is often the first to be listened to and has to be reassured before anyone else can be attended to; having noticed that, I can experiment with different dynamics that will help Anxiety to wait while others' concerns are heard.

Conclusion

In this chapter, I have presented reading and writing as ways of using written words to help us explore who we are. Much of what I have described is about the effectiveness of writing in helping us see ourselves, particularly by the mirror of reflective writing which places the self in a better plane of focus, so to speak. The self that appears is many-sided and engaged in a myriad of social relationships with other selves. I have tried to describe how writing helps us to distinguish our roles within this web of interactions, and insofar as when we write, we take one side of a conversation, we can also use writing to negotiate a place within that complex web, perhaps suggesting that the pen is mightier than the sword! But there is another conclusion that I would like to end with, which concerns you, the reader. Throughout the writing of this chapter, I have had you in mind. I don't know you, of course, but you have been essential to the process. The Self I have described is a socially determined construct; without a child, I cannot be a mother; without a listener, I cannot be in conversation. As the author of this chapter, I need a reader – so, over to you!

Further resources

For methods to get into writing, I have found the work of Peter Elbow to be enormously helpful. His early books *Writing without Teachers* (Oxford UP 1973) and *Writing with Power* (Oxford UP 1981) introduce the practice of free-writing; his later work gets us further into issues of composition, but still has a lot to say to us. See for example:

Elbow, P. (2000). *Everyone Can Write: Essays towards a hopeful theory of writing and teaching writing:* Oxford: Oxford UP.
Gillie Bolton has written extensively on reflective writing as an aid to personal development; see particularly
Bolton, G. (2010). *Reflective Practice: writing and professional development.* Third edition, London: Sage Publications.

There is substantial literature about the use of creative writing in therapy that is highly relevant to this chapter. The following contain some very useful material and suggestions for taking you further.

Bolton. G. (1999).*Therapeutic Potential of Creative Writing: writing myself.* London: Jessica Kingsley Publishers.
Hunt, C. and Sampson F. (eds) (1998). *The Self on the Page: theory and practice of creative writing in personal development.* London: Jessica Kingsley Publishers.
Bolton, G., Howlett S., Lago C., Wright J. (eds) (2004).*Writing Cures: an introductory handbook of writing in counselling and psychotherapy.* London: Routledge, 2004.

Although this last book is not about writing particularly, it sets the scene for how we can learn about ourselves from the shape of our lives, in this case from our possessions.

Gosling, S. (2008). *Snoop: what your stuff says about you.* London: Profile Books Ltd.

6
Developing through Music

Angela Harrison

The unease in the room was tangible. The eight group members stared studiously at the carpet as one by one they voiced their dissatisfaction at the piece of music they had just improvised. A sensation of chaos hung heavily in the air as the group recalled the succession of disjointed sounds made by tambourine, drum, bells, shaker, xylophone, triangle, bongos and hand chimes. Each player had been focused on their own activity, fiercely defending themselves against communication.

The comments came with unexpected clarity, identifying the shortfalls of the 'music' they had created.

'There was no rhythm to the music, nothing you could join in with or rely on'... 'Music is meant to have tunes and there was nothing but random sounds'... 'It was all so loud, there was no let up – I hated it'... 'It made me feel so childish'...and from others, just a grim silence.

I pondered for a moment. As the group's therapist and facilitator I was not there to provide solutions but to reflect back the observations of the group members for them to consider and process. But this felt like a crucial moment in the life of the group. Could we find a way to move forward that would help people already reeling from the effects of personal trauma to find meaning in the shared expression of their inner selves through music?

My response was to turn to each person and to refer to the element of music they had identified as missing. I gently encouraged them to hold that in their mind as they chose a new instrument and we then sat in awkward silence, the tension building, as we waited for the next piece to emerge.

The transformation was extraordinary. Underlying the gradual build-up of sound was a quiet yet reassuring pulse, played on a drum by the group member who had pointed out the lack of rhythm in the previous piece. With this firm base established, each player could join in at the moment they chose and make links with the rhythm, either matching it or weaving a complex dance around it. The skilled musician in the group who had identified the lack of 'tune' began to play, quietly at first, on the xylophone and a poignant melody captured the attention of those who were just beginning to shake or tap their instruments. The music rose and fell as the volume and energy drew people forward. The group self regulated the volume and the ebb and flow of emotional intensity formed a musical structure which was at the same time satisfying and intriguing. I sensed a reluctance to let the music go and the players vied with one another to 'have the last word' before falling back into quietness. As the memory of the last notes faded I saw, for the first time since the group had come together, a smile on the faces of one or two people. Even the most withdrawn were tentatively making eye contact across the room and the air felt clear and sweet.

Here music making that had been fragmented, unsatisfying and intolerable to many of the group members had transformed into music with style, variation and above all, meaning. Within the sounds created could be heard eight individual expressions of feelings, drawn together through rhythm and blended into a complete musical framework by wordless communication. The group members were able to identify the aspects of the initial improvisation which they found personally unsatisfying and then to change their contributions. With a subtle combination of individual responsibility and interdependence each player contributed their own strengths and so supported the playing of the others.

Interdependence is such an important aspect of life, I propose that without it we fail to grow and develop as individuals. This vignette has been constructed from a number of group situations I have encountered in my clinical practice and it not only describes one of those moments to be treasured in therapeutic work, but is a metaphor for life which will appear as a recurring motif amongst the themes to be explored in this chapter.

The content of this chapter is designed to give you an insight into different ways of thinking about musical experience and to equip you with ideas, not only for yourself, but for the sessions in your training or professional practice in which you are working with people who choose to express themselves by playing/referring to music or musical metaphor.

The first theme concerns collective musical experience. We are born into a world of sound, embedded in the musical traditions of our own culture. Music is a powerful means by which people assert their group identity. In our vignette, the members of the group connected with each other through a shared musical language, a collaborative endeavour.

Each player made an individual contribution, characterised by his or her personality and life experience but it was only in combination with the others that the music gained meaning.

The second theme looks at personal meaning in music. Moving from the group perspective we will examine the development of personality through the musical elements of mother/infant communication and the early interactions within a family group. This section will look at our personal experience of music and how this has influenced our choices at various stages of our lives. We will reflect on the catalysts which have sparked our interest in helping others through the professional role of counsellor/psychotherapist/music therapist. Through this and other examples it will become evident how music can play a role in shaping and retaining a sense of self.

The third theme explores communication with those around us. We have seen how the players in our group were initially intent on guarding their personal space, but began to communicate and move as 'one' through the second piece of music they created. In exploring these connections and the ways in which any group of musicians relate to one another in performance, we will seek to find parallels with the ways in which we all communicate in everyday life.

The conclusion returns to the concept of our 'inner group'. The opening chaotic piece revealed fragmented aspects of personality. Then, during a tension-filled silence, something changed. Each player found a voice which was prepared to speak out in the company of others. Earlier in this book, you have explored the many parts of yourself, including those hiding in the shadows, who struggle to make their voice heard. This final section will present ideas as to how you might support the process of transformation within yourself, by encouraging each of the characters in your 'inner group' to find a voice and to work together in a way which is creative and mutually supportive.

Collective musical experience

Music making as a means of developing cohesion and heightening awareness has been part of human experience since pre-history. Conard, Malina and Munzel (2009) describe how they found bone and ivory flutes in southwest Germany which demonstrate the presence of an established musical tradition at the time when modern humans colonized Europe, more than 35,000 years ago.

From these early beginnings, music has been integral to the development of different cultures by accompanying the rituals which make up everyday life. Rites of passage, celebrations, commemorations and collective endeavour all call for artistic expression including music, art, storytelling, dance and the sharing of specially prepared food. In any region in the world, variations in human temperament and the external environment are reflected in the myriad musical instruments, tonal systems and vocal styles which have evolved over time. The combination of these elements contributes to our sense of recognition. For example, folk music frequently uses rhythms taken from traditional dances, giving the melody a characteristic flavour. These pieces carry a resonance beyond the notes on the page and can evoke deep-seated feelings, often a collective 'wistfulness' encompassing past, present and future hopes.

Music may emanate from the individual mind of a composer or songwriter and yet it can excite a response in a diverse audience and remain fresh and relevant for succeeding generations. It has the capacity to draw together those who perform and those who listen into a collective emotional experience.

The recognition that music is so influential in people's lives has led to a harnessing of musical resources in order to achieve specific outcomes. Historically, music has been used as a means of stirring up the courage to enlist in the forces, to engage in warfare and to intimidate the enemy. In these times of intensive media involvement, music is also used to deepen the impact of political propaganda. This is in contrast to the restorative properties of music which can play their part in situations of conflict. Music can bring solace, for singing, playing and listening are all means of externalising inner experiences, distracting from fear, maintaining morale and establishing bonds.

The ability that music has to draw people together applies equally to our ordinary social interactions. In many towns and cities at night, the population separates itself out from the daytime configuration of home and work life and re-forms: the new groupings being determined not by social order, ethnicity, age or gender but predominantly by musical taste. People may opt for a 'quiet night in' or find themselves drawn to bars, pubs, night clubs, concert halls, cinemas, theatres, opera houses or a range of other places where music can be experienced and the tensions of everyday life forgotten. Music serves to meet, in all of us, the universal need to structure, express and manage the same basic human emotions.

In our search for meaning in our lives and in the world around us, religion and spirituality draw strongly on music to portray concepts which defy words. There is a need for some way of describing the numinous, and music, with its extraordinary range of variation in tone, timbre and quality can lift us above the everyday experience. Senses can be heightened and awareness of self can fade away. There can be great refreshment in time spent surrounded by uplifting sounds, smells and sights combined with episodes of quietness to calm and focus the mind. Silence is central to many spiritual practices and can provide the space and mental freedom to refresh and to generate new impetus and energy. Music, with all its variations, can help us to see ourselves and our concerns in a greater context.

When music is the common denominator, it is no longer so important whether people speak the same language or adhere to the same politics. In recent times, great musicians have made efforts to bring together players from across national, religious and social boundaries, notably in the Middle East and Ireland. Sir Georg Solti, for example, founded the World Orchestra for Peace in 1995. These conductors want to create a moment in time which demonstrates what can be possible when the self, with all its skill and individuality, is allowed to merge with other selves in a common experience. In the context of artistic endeavour the focus is on the extraordinary ability of humans to rise above individual concerns and to give themselves wholeheartedly for the edification of others.

This does not have to happen in some great arena or on a classical stage for it to have impact; cross-cultural music making may be entirely spontaneous and informal. I enjoy many different styles of music and have had moments in my life when music has connected me to others in a most unexpected but striking way. I remember a particular holiday in Spain with my husband when we called at a bar on the way back from a Flamenco show. In contrast to the formality of the stage show, the performers in the bar took time to assemble and as the music grew in intensity, led by the capable voice of the bar owner, all the patrons of the bar began to clap their own rhythms. We were thrilled to join in a collective musical experience which was not reliant on a shared language or culture, but on a resonance which went far deeper. What has been your experience? When I was thinking about this chapter, I found it useful to set aside some time to write down a list of shared moments in music which remain etched in my memory from early childhood, through my teenage years and onwards. You might like to try this also.

Points for reflection

Start by writing a list of occasions when music made an impact on you. You may want to include concerts, sports events, gigs and festivals, cinema, theatre or times with your family. It may help to create a time line and to jot down next to it the events that you can remember from each period.

What was the purpose of the music in this situation? Was it, for example, designed to change mood, encourage, reinforce loyalties, sell something or relax and refresh the mind?

Now you have your list, see whether it was the specific music that you remember or the impact that it had on you and on the people around you. Is there a connection between the significant moments you have listed?

Why do you think these were significant to you? Perhaps they resonated with some other experience and reminded you of a place, a person or an emotion? Perhaps they influenced subsequent decisions about your life? Or does their significance come from some quite different source?

Personal meaning in music

Personal meanings cannot, of course, be neatly separated from the cultural and collective contexts of our lives, but in this section the emphasis shifts towards the individual aspects of our musical experiences. Particular relationships and settings shape our musical abilities to hear and be heard, to sing and to compose. Our first relationship is with a mother or caregiver who, if all goes well, will nurture and satisfy our basic needs. While we are in the womb we are surrounded by the rhythms and sounds of our mother's body and once we are born, the interaction between us continues to have strong musical elements.

The vocabulary of our earliest reciprocal communications involves timing, imitation and anticipation. Vocal sounds can soothe, excite or amuse. The work of Colwyn Trevarthen (1979) has been to look at these early relationships in detail and he describes a process of 'co-regulation' in which a to-ing and fro-ing of sounds and expressions between mother and child is at play. Each responds to the other in a musical conversation without words. Daniel Stern (2004) speaks of an 'inter-subjective' experience in this interaction which plays an important role in the growing awareness of individual identity. The mother is providing her baby with regular feedback though 'mirroring' and empathy and it is by this process that a child begins to develop an understanding of self.

The opening vignette focused upon the group, but it can also illustrate this personal meaning of music. Meet Nicole, a fictitious client, characterised as the drummer in the improvisations.

Here she is, in a group of people participating in a 'shared' activity who seem oblivious to the contributions of anybody else. All Nicole can feel is her dissatisfaction with the situation in which she finds herself. She is aware of the violence with which she had been hitting the drum and feels a rush of angry thoughts as the terrifying coloured images of the past play out their familiar drama.

'No rhythm, no rhythm' pounds through Nicole's mind. As the chaos of the unrelated sounds comes to an end, she voices these thoughts in a venomous attack on the group's music. Where was the regular pulse that she was searching for?

Nicole finds the passivity of the therapist annoying. Surely she is there to help, and yet all she has done is to repeat back the words uttered by the members of the group. She has not offered to direct the group's musical contributions to ensure that everyone can get the sustenance they need.

Nicole retains her instrument for it now feels part of her and as a long silence falls on the group, she sits, brooding and bruised by her memories. Out of the silence comes the gentle resonance of a steady pulse and she sighs with relief and pleasure. Gradually she becomes aware of the sensations at the ends of her finger tips and realises that it is she who is playing the drum. Momentarily she looks up and meets the glance of the therapist. A silent exchange of understanding and knowledge passes across a room now alive with creativity.

The trauma experienced by this woman in her childhood has left its scars. Music, however, offers her a chance to vent the rage and indignation which could not be voiced at the time, in a wordless yet entirely dynamic form. It also offers the opportunity for nurturing and soothing. Nicole is perhaps instinctively seeking the reassuring rocking movements of a caring mother, and despite feeling let down by her own mother in the past, and the therapist in the present, she has become able to contribute that vital pulse for herself and the group.

In this case, Nicole was actively making music with the group, but insight can also be gained by listening. When we hear certain sounds, we can be transported back to a different time and environment. If you cast your mind back, can you remember some of the ways in which music and sound accompanied your childhood?

Maybe you can remember being sung to, or rocked with nursery songs. I have vivid memories of the records my mother used to play to occupy me while she got on with her work, and of the radio programmes we listened to together when I was preschool age. I have only to hear the sound of a particular clock tick, combined with the crackling of a fire in the hearth and memories come flooding back.

During my family's annual trip to the seaside, the whines of 'are we nearly there' and interminable travel sickness were deflected by singing – a lovely jumble of half-remembered words and tunes uniting us in a familiar ritual. Was this part of your experience? Maybe there were sounds which acted as signals – the chimes of the ice cream van or the theme tune to particular television programmes, perhaps. For me, a specific short whistle from my mother said 'bath time' and a system of coded messages played on the recorder enabled me to communicate with my friends who lived next door.

Points for reflection

What were your experiences? Spend a few minutes to think back to the places where you spent the most time as a young child. What could you hear?

Was there any live music? Do you remember singing or being sung to?

Do you remember the way music, or the lack of it, affected your reaction to places and people?

There is no longer a strong tradition of gathering round the piano or singing together in the home and for many, their first opportunity to make music comes at school. Some schools take pride in a good musical reputation, seeing benefit in the discipline required for mastering an instrument and performing together. In others, learning an instrument may not be valued or be rejected by peers as not being 'cool'. There are economic and social factors at play too. Not everyone has access to instrumental lessons and the cost of instrument hire/purchase and tuition can be prohibitive for many families, despite a number of initiatives to make such things accessible to all.

The musical environment of school can have a profound impact upon our relationship with music. Although for some it is enriching, many people that I encounter in my work had their confidence sapped as a child by thoughtless observations by staff on their musicality or by the cruelty of peers.

Adolescence is a particularly important time for building our relationship with music. It often becomes a key factor in the separation from parents and childhood into an emerging adult identity. Music is one of the most powerful influences to unite us with our peers and distance ourselves from the previous generation. Our relationships to the establishment and the family unit may change significantly as we begin to assert our preferences for style and values. The accompanying emotional upheaval often means that as adults we can recall the soundtrack of our adolescence more readily than at any other period of our lives. The impact is often underlined because we frequently 'lived' the music by abandoning ourselves to its rhythm in dance.

Points for reflection

What was your experience of music in your school years?

Did you sing or play an instrument? Were you part of a choir or group or ensemble?

What are the feelings you associate with this as you look back?

What part did music play for you as a teenager? Is it easy to recall tunes and lyrics from that period? Do you have any reaction when you hear this music now?

Have your tastes changed?

As adults we may continue to socialise with those who share our musical preferences or we may seek out new musical experiences. However, sometimes we seem to have little choice about what we listen to. There are few moments in a day when there is not some music to be heard. When we wake to the radio alarm or switch on the television we are immediately bombarded by sound. Programmes of all kinds are accompanied by background music and adverts are full of jingles and catch phrases designed to help to embed them in our memories. How many hours are spent in our lives listening to various forms of electronic music while 'on hold' on the telephone? We may take it for granted, but we cannot escape the piped music in shops, public areas and recreation centres. We have music in our cars, our phones, our personal music systems and computers: we can hear other people's music on buses and tubes, trains and planes. The danger is that we become desensitised and the true power of music to stir our emotions, stimulate memories and to energise can be lost.

Are we, like those in the vignette, able to identify the musical aspects which are unsatisfying and substitute an experience which is enriching, not only for ourselves but for others? There is now the potential to carry round with us a vast collection of music, a sort of 'portable identity', which acts as a resource for all eventualities. We can, without the help of anyone else, alter our heart, pulse and breathing rate, as well as change our mood simply by putting in ear phones and slipping into a private world.

This may be a form of escapism, or it may be a necessary way of giving ourselves some space. Another possibility is that we can view our music collection as having been chosen in response to certain needs within ourselves and so by looking at the content, we can see the ways in which the music we choose to listen to reflects our personal experiences or attributes.

Points for reflection

To learn more, you might like to try this. Make a list of the music which has been important to you in the different stages of your life and the music which you choose to listen to or play now. You may want to refer to the time line you created earlier.

Bring each piece of music to mind and write down the feelings you associate with each one. Is there a specific experience that it brings to mind? Can you associate it with an attribute or characteristic?

Jot down the attribute next to each piece until you have built up a full picture.

Look at the attributes and see whether or to what extent they are component parts of your character. Are they all familiar or do any seem 'not like' you?

It may help to see some of my examples:

'An Innocent Man' by Billy Joel seems to reverberate with my love of risk taking. Parts of the 'Italian Symphony' by Mendelssohn stir childlike excitement. 'All Right Now' by Free was important in my teens and reflects insecurity about my own value. The 'Alpine Symphony' by Richard Strauss gives me a heady sense of courage in adversity.

As I look through my list, it is clear that my most loved pieces do indeed reflect aspects of my character which are familiar and recognisable. However, I want to return to this activity in the conclusion, for the unfamiliar is also significant.

Communicating with others

As you will discover, whether you are currently training or already qualified, central to our role in a listening profession is the complex business of communication. The language of the therapeutic encounter is made up of sounds, rhythm, tonality, body movements and silence. With our clients, we know that we are to attend not only to the spoken, but to the unspoken. Music can speak to us with or without the help of words, at times bypassing thought to reach straight to the heart. So it may be valuable at this point to look at *how* and *what* is communicated through music.

Communication can take place through actively playing but also through gesture and eye contact. When instrumental players or singers rehearse, they learn to use all available nonverbal cues to share the responsibilities of performance from the very first moment. There may be an audible 'count in' which would set the tempo, but more often than not the start point is conveyed through a paced intake of breath, a subtle gesture or a glance. As the music takes shape, there may be indications of changes in speed or in who is leading which may again be communicated through eye contact or body movement. The musical line may be passed between the players and the interchangeable flow of initiating and following can be seen to resemble the early mother/ infant interaction that was discussed earlier.

This does not only apply to professional musicians. Whenever I run an improvisation workshop for non-musicians, I always emphasise that there is no 'wrong' in the equation. Rather than being a test of skill, music-making in this context is all about communication. It is about exchanged glances, matching one another's rhythms, copying different styles, laughter and the sheer joy of creating something together which is totally unexpected in its form. Afterwards, people describe great relief that the process had been non-judgemental and liberating and find that it can provide insight into new ways of relating to others.

Musicians can convey an added dimension, however. Music can convey mood states, both through the use of words and through tonality, tempo and style. In addition, a personal connection can be made with the listener through the commitment of the musician to 'speak' through their voice or instrument. A performer will draw from his or her own internal world in order to characterize the music, and a high level of proficiency on an instrument does not guarantee this ability to communicate through the music. I remember vividly my viola teacher demonstrating this during a master class. He performed a short piece with technical accuracy, presenting exactly what was written on the page. The sound was beautiful.

He then paused and said, "Now, I will put myself into it" and played the same piece again. His body language changed, leaning towards us and making eye contact, moving freely with the shape of the musical phrases. He was able to convey emotion and meaning through the instrument in a free flow of flexible timing and energy. This time, the sound was not only beautiful but 'spoke' to each of us in a powerful way, the character of the player blending with the intention of the composer and meeting each listener in a new encounter.

This understanding of the extra dimension a performer adds to a piece of composed music is described by Daniel Levitin (2006). He talks about the link between variability of the beat in music and that of the beat of life as it is lived and the pleasurable exercise in the brain of synchronising with the beat of the music.

There are parallels here in the subtleties of communication between therapists and clients. The human voice is the most obvious instrument that we possess, and our abilities to make use of its range and tonal variations are important skills in connecting with others. Our voice and the way we use it is the most personal part of our communications, and we can 'put ourselves into it', as in the example above, or withhold. Similarly, we can understand a lot by listening carefully to our clients' voices. We need to be able to hear whether or not the client is 'in' the voice, and recognise when the words say one thing but the tone of voice another. Much of therapeutic work involves facilitating or enabling the client to develop their own voice, and to be able to hear themselves and others.

In my work as a therapist, I frequently encounter children who are severely delayed in their development or who are on the autistic spectrum. These children are likely to have been referred to a music therapist as opposed to other talking interventions because their poor level of understanding and use of language means that they cannot express themselves verbally.

They come to the therapy space for the first time and see an array of colourful instruments laid around the room. I greet them with a song they will soon know so well, as I start and end each session with the same tune using simple words. I may then give a basic explanation as to the purpose of our meeting and say that the instruments are there for them to explore and within the boundaries of safety, 'whatever you do is right'.

Now for some children this presents a thrilling Aladdin's Cave of possibilities. They will rush from instrument to instrument, pulling, banging, jangling and throwing, drawing as much sound out as quickly as possible. They are likely to be oblivious to my musical contribution and eager to use me only as a means of extending their physical capability, for example, taking hold of my hands to make them play the piano as they wish. With this level of enthusiasm and interaction with the instruments there is the potential over a period of time for the child to begin to listen, to hear my music and to find opportunities for musical turn taking. So the embryonic stages of language exchange will develop and flourish. The mutual communication made through musical sounds can be sufficiently satisfying to encourage new levels of interaction with other people in the child's life and this will impact all aspects of learning and social life.

There are other children who come into the room and present themselves as quite unreachable. The fact that they remain in the room is my one indication of hope for the therapeutic process as it has become evident over the years that such children will leave if they do not wish to be there. The child will show no obvious interest in the instruments, even less in me as a person and will move around the room in an impermeable "bubble" from which my sounds and intentions to communicate are bounced back unacknowledged.

Alec is a boy with autism who on first meeting presented as 'unreachable'. He did not make eye contact, shunned my attempts to play familiar music yet remained in the therapy room, rocking or tapping beaters. He had been referred to me because of distressing mood swings, and being unable to use language, he could not explain what was happening. After several fruitless attempts, I finally found a way of making a connection. I sat at the piano and improvised a 'soundtrack' which picked up on the rhythm and mood of Alec's actions. When he jumped around the room, the music became lively; when he rocked on the chair the sounds were rhythmic and soothing. Several weeks later, from across the room Alec heard me sing his name in a very long single breath. He looked across and met my eye for the first time since the therapy began. He clapped his hands, laughing and rushed over to clap my hands for me. From this point, Alec and I moved into a more balanced relationship in which we could both play instruments, take turns and share.

Alec gained from the therapeutic relationship a stronger sense of self and with it a new confidence in his interactions with others. Unlike the majority of people coming to a therapist or counsellor, he did not have the option to use words to communicate. It is easy to overlook the power of non-verbal communication for those working with language. Music can provide a means of exploring this in a playful and enjoyable way so you might like to experiment with the following activities.

Points for reflection

Get together with friends and experiment with communication on instruments. Maybe start by using drums to have a conversation in pairs. If you have no instruments, improvise with cutlery, cereal packets, coffee beans – whatever you can find that makes a sound!

Put on a piece of music you all enjoy. See if you can create an accompaniment using everyday items to tap, hit or rattle. How are you keeping in touch with one another?

Share the experience in words and talk about what was communicated, misunderstood or enriched by the very different vocabulary.

Bringing it together

Music enables us to communicate with others in a form which transcends words. This does not only apply to those who play or sing, for when we speak of being 'on the same wavelength', 'in harmony with' or 'singing from the same song sheet', we are of course using the rich language of music to describe qualities of human interaction. When we empathise, there is something in us which literally resonates with an aspect of the other.

In the same way, different styles of music reverberate with the many facets of our personality and create a unique 'blueprint' which remains intact even when other faculties fail. When a person has dementia, for example, there is evidence that music can continue to evoke memories and a sense of identity when other aspects of life may be fragmented. There have been many moving occasions in my work when music has helped older people to access memories and has temporarily restored their 'voice'. However, we can discover more about our own voices and musical blueprint at any stage in our lives. Throughout this book, you have been offered a glimpse of your own 'inner voices' from a number of different perspectives. How might you recognise the different aspects of yourself through music?

Why not bring these characters now into the music therapy room, show them the circle of chairs and suggest that they sit wherever they like? You can use your imagination to equip each of them with a choice of instrument, experiment with ideas as to the style in which they might play and then watch and listen. You will have gained sufficient understanding of the process to assess what may be needed in order to reassure the painfully shy, encourage the uncertain, empathise with the wounded and temper the more dominant influences.

Points for reflection

Draw out a plan of your inner music group, with plenty of space for comments and ideas.

On the basis of what you know about each character, make a note of the musical instruments that would appeal to them (there is a limitless supply available).Then see if you can imagine the sounds they might make. If you have actual instruments in the house, you can always experiment as you go along.

How will the group inter-relate? Are there members of your group who would hate to be in this situation? Why do you think this is? Who might really enjoy it?

Who would take the lead? Would they be challenged? Who will start the improvisation and who will hold back?

Is there a character who would facilitate rather than take control?

An earlier activity in this chapter invited you to think about the attributes that were associated with your favourite pieces of music. For me it revealed not only the connections between how I see myself and the characteristics of the music, but also the extent to which I have neglected so many musical styles. Where is the rock, the hip hop, the jazz, electronic music, folk, baroque, choral music, improvisation, blues and world music? Could it be that these are linked to areas of myself that I also choose to neglect? If my own musical ensemble is to have balance, then I need to bring new instruments into the group. Perhaps you would also find it rewarding to see whether you can identify any of the characters who have yet to join in with your group.

With an inner group assembled, can we now find harmony? Looking beyond a popular image of amiable companionship, I suggest that harmony requires courage to bring together different elements into a cohesive whole, withstanding the inevitable dissonances. As in the keyboard inventions of J S Bach, if any note is abandoned because it 'does not fit' or because it is too difficult to play, a moment of tension is avoided but also the possibility of the sweetness of resolution. To allow all the parts of ourselves to 'stand their ground' and be accepted for the integral role they play takes nerve but brings its own rewards.

Self reflection is a lifelong activity and particularly essential for those who are entering or already involved in supporting the psychological and emotional development of others. One of the great joys of music is that there are always new discoveries to be made. A chance hearing of a piece on the radio or a new singer in the charts can change the course of our development. More than this, there is music in each of us. Rhythm accompanies our lives from the moment we come into being, and our heartbeat, breathing and the dynamic movement of our limbs continue to echo the life affirming pulse. We thrive on the rhythm of day and night, work and rest, and our relationships with others have an ebb and flow which mirror the early interactions of our infancy.

Deprived of this musicality, literal or metaphorical, we would be little more than a collection of isolated, disjointed sounds, as described in the opening of this chapter. We need music, or in the words of Yehudi Menuhin, 'Music is like earth, air, fire and water, a great basic element that belongs everywhere; like bread and compassion, mankind cannot live without it ....'

Further resources

Books about music and the brain:

Sacks, O. (2007). *Musicophilia*. London: Picador, Pan Macmillan Ltd.
Mithen, S. (2005). *The Singing Neanderthals*. London: Phoenix, Orion Books Ltd.
Malloch, S. and Trevarthen, C. (ed). (2009). *Communicative Musicality*. Oxford: Oxford University Press.

Autobiographies of musicians:

Tillis, M. (1960). *Chords and Discords*. London: Phoenix.
Garrett, L. (2001). *Notes from a Small Soprano*. London: Hodder and Stoughton.

An academic and a fictional account of music therapy practice:

Darnley-Smith, R. and Patey, H M. (2003). *Music Therapy*. London: Sage Publications.
Picoult, J. (2011). *Sing You Home*. London: Hodder and Stoughton.

Films:

Cosi. (1996). Dir: Mark Joffe.
The Chorus. (2004). Dir: Christophe Barratier.
Little Voice. (1998). Dir: Mark Herman.

To Play and to Fight (Tocar y Luchar). (2006). Dir: Alberto Arvelo Mendoza.
The School of Rock. (2003). Dir: Richard Linklater.

Relevant websites:

www.cultureandwellbeing.org.uk
www.bamt.org
www.musicmindspirit.org

All of these have inspired and led me on in my own quest for self-awareness. While they may not carry the same meaning for you, I hope that some will act as a catalyst in your search.

7
Developing through Visual Imagery

Elizabeth Ashby

Visual imagery helps us make sense of our world and it is a fundamental component of our sense of self. Our development is intimately connected to what we see. As babies we learn rapidly to recognize and distinguish human faces, helping us to build the relationships that are vital to our survival. The ability to manipulate objects and reach developmental milestones such as sitting and walking are significantly affected by sight. From these early experiences through to the present moment, visual images are inseparably bound up with our development. The importance of the visual all around us and our engagement with it are integral aspects of our lives, expressed in the way we dress, what we find attractive, what we delight in, how we learn and more.

Our engagement with visual imagery takes many forms and is experienced on multiple levels as we grow and develop. On one level, our early attempts at making marks develop to become an ability to symbolize and communicate ideas in two- and three-dimensional images. These abilities become ever more complex and greatly aid our learning through childhood. We learn that different sorts of images convey different messages – a computer-generated presentation can communicate ideas in words and pictures, but may be very different in its purpose to the paintings in a national gallery.

At another level we communicate what we want the world to know about us through the visual aspect of our self image, which develops as we grow and change through childhood, adolescence and adulthood. We use colours, textures, shapes and forms to present ourselves to the world and to evaluate the presentations of others. Colour and visual imagery are fundamental to every aspect of our lives, impacting upon us through the natural world around us, through public and environmental design, the way we decorate our homes and the products we buy and use in everyday life. We live in a fast-developing world that engages with our visual and symbolic capacity in many ways. Our self image is shaped and conditioned by our own visual culture and its impact on us is powerful, resonating deeply within us, whether or not we consciously engage with and appreciate our cultural heritage.

This chapter looks at the use of visual imagery for self exploration from two main perspectives. It provides a way of reflecting on ourselves and aspects of our lives that facilitates the accessing of unconscious material that can be brought into awareness. It also offers a means of self expression, using image-making to express emotions, provide containment and facilitate play.

The store of images

Each individual develops over time an internal image bank which contains a vast store of diverse images we can draw on when engaging in image-making. Visual images, scenes and experiences spanning our lives from our earliest moments to the present are stored as memories, forming the basis of our adult appreciation of the world. Many of these images will reflect our particular cultural heritage and our individuality and will be sources of pleasure, giving us a sense of belonging and contributing to our sense of self.

These first activities introduce you to the idea of tapping into your visual memory and becoming more aware of your own image bank.

Points for reflection

Read through this list of well-known places and see if you can picture them in your mind.

Eiffel Tower	Niagara Falls
Taj Mahal	Sydney Opera House
London Eye	Statue of Liberty
Grand Canyon	Great Wall of China

Now try these –

'Mona Lisa'	Marge Simpson
Darth Vader	'The Scream'
Humphrey Bogart	Marilyn Munroe
'The Hay Wain'	Nelson Mandela
'Guernica'	Donald Duck

What images can you locate in your internal image bank? Different cultures may have very different images. You may, for example, have a store of religious images, landscapes, animals, plants, machines, flags, trademarks, maps, stamps – and so on.

For many, family photographs are highly significant. Can you see any in your mind's eye? Often photographs come to replace memories of events or people, and we carry them around with us in an internal album.

Images are not often emotionally neutral, but are associated with certain feelings and thoughts. These are not all benign. We may have disturbing images in our store that conjure up memories we would rather leave undisturbed. It is not necessary to open any 'albums' that you are in any way apprehensive about. It is enough to register their presence and move on, for the point of the activity is to become aware of the extent of the store from which we draw upon in our visual imagination.

Making images for self exploration

The artist Georgia O'Keefe (1926) said 'I found I could say things with colours and shapes which I couldn't say in any other way – things I had no words for' and in my opinion this is true for all who are willing to create images and explore what lies within. I am an art psychotherapist and my work involves enabling clients to deepen their insight into their inner worlds.

Making images can enable individuals to gain access to unconscious material which otherwise remains beyond conscious awareness. Image-making can take the artist/client to a liminal experience – that is, one on the threshold of consciousness. It has been compared to dreaming while awake. Artists prepare to make a picture or construction with perhaps only a vague idea of what they want to make or how to make it. They allow their mind to wander freely, not trying to produce anything in particular but allowing the materials to speak back to them as they work. In some ways similar to free association, it is a process that is not consciously directed but allowed to develop almost with a life of its own, revealing itself to its creator as the image unfolds.

Such images may be like 'Freudian slips' in which the image emerges contrary to the artist's conscious intention. One client painted a boat sailing to an island to rescue her father, but in the picture the boat is going in the opposite direction and her face looks away from the stated destination. The image enabled her to see the conflict between her conscious wishes and her hidden feelings, which could then be explored productively in therapy.

When we are not distracted by thoughts crowding in on us and are able to give ourselves to the moment of creation, we can find ourselves in a dialogue with our image. Many artists are surprised by the image that is revealed as they engage with the materials. The created object speaks back to its creator and each is influenced by the other; thus the artist becomes participant, witness and observer within the process.

An art therapist who was reflecting on the death of her father was quietly working with a piece of clay. The clay felt soothing, and almost without realizing it the therapist found that she had made an image of her father that reflected his characteristics. In her engagement with this image she was reminded of a conversation with her father before his death and found herself making an image of herself in that situation. The first figure of her father seemed to speak to her, and thus the second figure of herself emerged from the clay in answer to the first. She, the creator, had participated in making those images and then found herself engaged in a process almost outside and yet not outside herself. She experienced herself in three roles, representing her father, herself and at the same time witnessing the process. It was a powerful and healing encounter and an important moment in the grieving process for her.

Artistic media

Different artistic media lend themselves to different types of imagery. Art psychotherapist Schaverien (1992) introduced the concept of distinct types of therapeutic imagery. Although the boundary between them is not rigid, the distinction can be helpful. 'Diagrammatic' imagery is that which is narrative and explanatory but does not contain obvious emotion, whereas an 'embodied' image is one that is full of emotion that can be seen and felt by the creator and observer. Pencils, felt pens, markers and crayons generally produce cleaner lines and are useful for making diagrammatic imagery. 'Messier' materials, such as paint, charcoal, pastels and clay lend themselves to more emotionally expressive images.

The range of feelings expressed in artwork is influenced by the materials that are used. The eye, brain and body all respond to the properties of the materials. The texture, the intensity, the smell, the colours and the feel of the materials contribute to the creation of the image and its expressiveness. In addition, the physical sensation of the method being used has an impact on the artist's whole being; the feeling of careful methodical drawing with pencils is quite qualitatively different to that of painting on a large canvas with oils or drawing expansively with charcoal and pastels or making three-dimensional images with clay. Added to this is the feel of the equipment used by the artist – the brushes, sculpting tools, easels and so on, which contribute to the physical engagement with the image-making process.

The more comfortable the artist is with the materials, the environment and the equipment, the more conducive the situation is for working with one's emotions and unconscious. Then it becomes more possible to lose oneself within the process for a time and experience that quality of liminality that pushes the boundaries of consciousness during the creative act.

Two basic approaches to image-making are those of abstract and figurative imagery. Figurative art attempts to represent what is seen as accurately as possible using artistic media, while abstract art allows you to work with colour and shape in whatever manner you choose. There is value in both approaches, and they can also be combined. Some people are not comfortable making abstract images because this approach is unfamiliar to them, while others are not comfortable making representational images because they do not feel sufficiently skilled. Art therapists encourage their clients to work in whatever way feels most helpful without being concerned about their level of ability, and in the context of trying the activities in this chapter I would encourage you to let go of any fears and prejudices you may have left over from school days and just experiment with the media.

Before you begin, however, it is prudent to be thoughtful about your own experience. We are constantly drawing upon our own stored images and reworking them into new and unique forms. Some of us will have images in our internal bank of difficult and distressing experiences, and care must be taken when accessing such material because it is possible to be re-traumatized by particularly vivid scenes. In these circumstances it may be helpful to work through this material with an art psychotherapist. In art therapy, the therapist takes care of images within the safety and containment of the therapeutic space and relationship, so that the creator can leave having experienced catharsis and the relief that accompanies the process.

Most of the suggested activities can be done alone or with others. Working with a trusted friend can offer possibilities of support and containment, a richer conversation, a deepening relationship and more fun!

Exploring the image

Janet's image

The image above was created by a trainee drama therapist, Janet, who told me about her picture.

'My best friend, Sarah, has become bulimic and I am really worried about her. I suspected something was going on when we shared a flat and she would spend ages in the bathroom, and obviously she was throwing up. That's why there's a toilet on the left of my picture, with food round it.'

'Is that Sarah in the picture?' I asked Janet.

'Yes, that's Sarah, and she has no mouth because she won't talk to me about anything. It's like she is under a big black cloud that is raining. The marks on her arms are cuts, because she is self-harming, which I am really worried about. And she's writing about that stuff in her course work as if it is all OK, which is why there are two drama masks and a question mark, because I really wonder how seriously she is taking the work for her theatre degree.'

'The situation sounds really difficult. There's a lot going on round Sarah in your picture. Can you tell me a bit more about it?'

She said, *'The hand coming towards her is me, but she has told me to 'back off' so I feel 'lost', like the sign says. In the bubble above my hand are all her other friends who are crying and she is shutting them out too. Under my hand is a world going round, as it is, unaware of all of these problems, everything around us is just going on as if nothing is happening.'*

At first Janet is describing and explaining to me the features of her drawing in quite a literal manner, as if it is a diagram of a situation. She is obviously upset, however, so it is not the case that the image contains little emotion.

'The lost feelings and the empty space on your side of the picture are huge; do they relate to other aspects of your life as well?'

With some gentle encouragement we were able to explore further. Janet and Sarah had been extremely close, and she felt the loss of her friend very sharply. On reflection, she thought that her lost feelings could also be related to feelings about her family.

'Last year my brother had a huge row with my parents and moved out. I've tried to contact him but he doesn't want to know – I guess that's a big 'back off' ...... and my Mum and Dad just won't talk about him, so there is this big empty space... I still feel so upset about it. Having a close friend has been really important to me since my brother left, so losing Janet has been very difficult for me.'

Until she made the image Janet had felt completely overwhelmed by the situation.

The picture enabled her to understand the depth of her own feelings and then to think about how to help her friend Sarah. It demonstrated the power of the image even in diagrammatic form to facilitate learning and change.

You might try the next activity either on your own or with a friend or colleague. Someone else's perspective can be valuable in learning to appreciate the many different levels of understanding that images can contain.

Points for reflection

Try to obtain lead pencils of different drawing strengths (such as B, B2, B4 and B6), a rubber, some coloured pencils and paper not smaller than A4.

Find a suitable space to work in and choose a time of day when you will not be interrupted for a reasonable length of time.

Consider making an image of a particular situation in your personal life that has been on your mind or needs some reflection, attempting to think creatively about it and allowing your mind to wander around the ideas you are trying to explore. Draw it as clearly as possible on the paper, using the pencils to make lighter or darker marks.

You can combine images and words in your picture if that is helpful, but do not worry about how your picture will turn out. Draw for about 20 minutes and stop when you feel it is complete.

When you are happy that you have finished, spend 10 to 15 minutes reflecting on the image you have produced. If you have worked alone, try speaking to the image and talking yourself through the different aspects it reveals. If you have done this with a friend, talk together about your images, taking it in turns to discuss each other's material. Images can be very effective in drawing our attention to aspects that our conscious minds have overlooked.

Ellie's image

The next image facilitates an exploration of the inner world of a newly qualified art therapist called Ellie, who kindly allowed me to share this picture made in personal therapy. Ellie's picture is made with messier materials– in this case charcoal– allowing her much more freedom of expression of her emotions as well as helping her to explore her feelings about a situation. Ellie told me that the picture was about her relationship with her absent father and she explained her picture to me.

I asked Ellie to tell me about what was going on in the dark panel. She told me it was a very nasty space, very frightening and very angry, but that she felt she had worked through those feelings and was in a better place now.

She said *'The dark panel on the right represents my past experience of the situation with my Dad, and the main body of the picture is about my current thoughts.'*

'Who is the central figure?' I asked her.

'He is my father. He has been very stupid so I gave him a jester's hat and, because he has been out of my life for a few years he has a face that has no detail except for clown-like eyes. I drew him like a sort of scarecrow-type stick figure, standing in the mess he has created surrounded by whirlwinds, which is how it felt to me.'

'What's that below him?'

'It's a bed of nails,' Ellie said, *'and it's what he deserves! On the left of the bed of nails is a pile of vomit (my feelings about what he has done), and there is a barking dog and a fierce bear (I know it doesn't really look like one, but it is!) which represent more angry feelings – mine and other people's.'*

'The main body of the picture looks like a stage, with a hint of a curtain around the top,' I suggested, and Ellie agreed.

'This is the drama of my life and my problems with my Dad. The figures below the curtain, sort of in the sky, looking all angry with teeth,

shouting and with angry eyes, are other people looking down on him, shouting at him. They are also me shouting at him.' She paused for a moment.

'And I think on another level, the jester is me too, because I feel he made a fool of me.'

I wondered about the snake and the other two things coming out of the spectre on the right's mouth. Ellie said 'The snake has deceived him, the thing with five tails is a whip scourging him and the funny animal is a weasel, another deceiving sort of animal.'

'Who are the two little figures below the weasel?' I asked.

'They are me. The one above is me in chains, all tied up feeling terrible. And the person below is me with the chains falling off, in the light. It's me being released from the pain and anger I have been feeling.'

'In the picture you have represented yourself as a really small character compared to the jester.'

Ellie replied 'I hadn't seen that before, and you are right. I look far too small and vulnerable.'

'I wonder if you could think of a way to change the balance.'

'Yes, I am going to make another image that reverses the balance and makes me large and the jester very small and insignificant, and I am going to put him in a box in a corner of a room where he can't disturb my life too much.'

This picture very powerfully conveys Ellie's feelings and the ongoing journey in her relationship both with her father and with herself. She told me that she felt a great sense of release after making it and felt that her second picture would move her on again.

Ellie's picture has shown how she was able to use the drawing process to both explore her inner world on several levels, and also to express her powerful feelings about the situation. This is more of an 'embodied' image than the first, as the emotion is more evident. The picture shows how many aspects of a situation can coexist simultaneously in one image, representing different levels of thoughts and feelings, and how parts of the pictures can mean different things at different times.

Many images will be useful for both discovering aspects of one's experience which were not previously available for conscious processing and to express feelings. The next activity gives you an opportunity to try and create an embodied image for yourself and see what happens.

Points for reflection

Gather some messier materials, such as paint, pastels or charcoal, and again find a suitable time and space to work in. You may feel you wish to do this alone or with a friend. Try to get into a meditative mood to enable the image to unfold in your mind and onto the paper, and try to express your thoughts and feelings about some aspect, relationship or situation in your personal life that puzzles or troubles you. Give yourself longer to make this image, perhaps 45 minutes, and try to become lost in the process, unaware of time passing and in tune with the materials. It will probably take some practice at this process for you to feel comfortable enough not to censor yourself, but it is worth persisting.

When you feel the image is complete prop it up to make it easier to see, and reflect on what has emerged in the image. Think about the impact it had on you while you were making it. If you have done this with a friend, talk about the process together – what you experienced while making the image and what you see in the completed picture. The aim is not to show how much artistic talent you can display but to allow your creativity to reveal elements of understanding that could not be gained by simply talking about it. Ask questions about the different parts of the picture and the different levels they operate on, and try and draw out the subtleties of the image you have created, letting them speak to you.

Image making to transform mood

Image-making can be both very stimulating and very soothing, depending on the choice of subject and materials. Image-making can be used to purposefully transform mood, an aim I exploit when working with chronically depressed clients who can find enjoyment outside of their normal experience when engaged in artwork.

An image can be a vehicle for the expression and containment of otherwise overwhelming feelings and may provide a means for the evacuation of such emotions in catharsis. Clients who are very distressed because of events in their lives such as bereavement, betrayal or trauma need to express and then to evacuate those overwhelming feelings. This can lead to a sense of mastery by externalising an internal experience of significance to the creator.

One elderly lady I worked with, who felt tremendous anger towards her former partner because of the abusive control he had had over her, felt enormous relief when she was encouraged to make large images onto which she squirted ready-mix poster paint straight from the bottle. This allowed her to make expansive images that expressed how she was feeling, and if the painting alone did not bring the necessary relief, then stamping on the image and scraping the paint with a fork did have the desired effect.

Another, who was virtually blind, found great comfort in making an object like a shoe which was reminiscent of her days as a young woman. She was not so keen on the sensation of the damp clay, but was excited by the changes in her shoe object when it was biscuit-fired, and then really delighted when, glazed and fired again, it became smooth, shiny and colourful. This making of the object also represented stages of her life, and had great significance for her.

Points for reflection

The aim of this activity is to express strong emotions through working with clay. Clay is a medium that is extremely valuable because of its three-dimensional and physical qualities; it is useful for catharsis because it can be treated harshly but later can still be used to produce a transformational image. It can become something useful such as a pot or other domestic object, or an imaginative image, such as an abstract convolution of shapes or a scene with people or animals; the possibilities are endless. As before, ensure that the surroundings and timing are conducive to this exercise and think about the strong emotions you need to release.

Choose a piece of clay roughly the size of your fist and start to knead it in your hands and on your work surface, in a similar manner to making bread, knocking the air out of it and making the clay malleable. This approach is ideal for expressing strong emotions, such as anger and grief, and gives time for reflection on the situation that resulted in you feeling this way. Consider what the feeling means for you; how it came about, what might be significant about it. If you can become thoroughly absorbed in the process you will find your unconscious material more accessible. The act of kneading the clay can be a strong physical exertion, or more gentle and soothing.

Once the clay is malleable start to manipulate it to make the image you have in your mind. Give yourself a reasonable amount of time to make your image, and imagine pushing the strong emotions into the clay as you work with it and experience your reaction.

When you feel it is ready, sit back and explore the object that you have made. Note how the process of making it felt to you and what thoughts arose. What can you see in the image that surprises you? What impact does the finished object have on you, and what questions does it open up? If you have done this exercise with a friend discuss what the impact is on the observer as compared to the creator.

Creative supervision

In the context of my work I have engaged in creative supervision both as client and as facilitator, and have found it a very helpful process as a tool for reflection and for problem-solving. The group is facilitated by an art therapist in a studio setting and provides an opportunity for the members to bring aspects of their work with clients for supervision in a creative context. It consists of about six psychologists, counsellors and trainees who all work with clients and usually lasts for two hours. The members have the opportunity to explore the art therapy studio and to become familiar with its contents and the materials, and they are then invited to depict pictorially the client material they would like to explore.

The participants usually find the images they produce quite surprising. However they choose to depict the situation, whether diagrammatically, or using more emotive artistic media such as paint, pastels or charcoal, or as a three-dimensional sculpture or construction, each image contains key information about that client and the work the member is engaged in. They experience the image on a number of levels, finding themselves in different roles such as those of creator, participant and witness.

Considerably more understanding of the situation is gained from the combined consideration by all members of the group. Generally the group participants leave the session with an enhanced understanding, a sense of having been heard and of not being alone with their issues, and the sense of relief that may come from this shared experience. Members of the group can choose whether to take their images with them, or leave the more disturbing ones with the therapist for containment.

Mary's image

This painting was made during a creative supervision session by a therapist, Mary, who wanted to think about her client's story. She has drawn the client in the centre, with her depressed aunt on the right, and her boyfriend on the left. The client had become attached to the boyfriend and then discovered his capacity for domestic violence.

Mary told the group how '*all these aspects are in my picture, but the more I looked at it the more I realized that each person I painted also represents different and contradictory aspects of my client herself. She can be very thoughtful and concerned for others, but also has a tendency towards depression, though not to the extent of her aunt. When she feels very angry about things she wants to throw stuff and break things. She is not proud of the times when she has done that and then is very self-critical about her lack of control, but knows she is mirroring behaviour she witnessed as a child.*'

Seeing this in her image surprised Mary, but she was also uncomfortably aware of recognizing aspects of herself in the figures too. Like her client, she realized that there were elements of her own life that needed changing, and that she was resisting facing them because it felt too difficult. One of the group members asked her about the eye in the picture.

Mary's thought was that the eye represented the paranoia that the client experienced. I wondered whether it perhaps represented some other things too. As Mary and the group thought about it, they felt the eye also represented a means of escape to a different world. It could also represent a spiritual awakening in the client. For Mary herself it meant that she needed to open her eyes to those problems of her own that resonated with her client's materials.

We can see from this example how one image can be seen to contain both conscious and unconscious material which can then be explored. Different and contradictory aspects of the self can be manifested in a single artwork and contained within it.

Points for reflection

You could try this with a group of colleagues at work. Gather together some basic art materials, bearing in mind the setting in which you will be working and what resources you can access. Each participant chooses the subject of some client work they are currently engaged in which they wish to reflect on, and makes an image in the first part of the session. When all the participants have finished their artwork, spend some time quietly reflecting on your own image, what you felt while you were making it, how you feel now, what issues were raised by the process and so on. Then, taking it in turns, discuss each image, starting with the creator's thoughts on it and then opening the discussion to the other participants. You may find that the process enables much creative thinking to take place and greater insight to be gained than by discussion alone.

Taking care of ourselves

The work of counsellors and therapists exposes them to the emotional distress of others and this can have a considerable impact, as can aspects of the employing organization such as working conditions and funding issues. Looking after ourselves is an important aspect of our self awareness that we need to address honestly and adequately if we are to continue to practise and thrive. It is important for us as professionals to find ways of nurturing our own needs, and image-making for ourselves can be an important aspect of our self care.

The emotional residue of sessions can continue to impact the therapist for some time after the session and processing the experience in image-making can allow for reflection and working through, and may give us a different way of viewing the impact of the work. In addition to helping us to process our counter-transference reactions and developing our understanding of the material, the containment afforded by the image can allow the creator to leave much of the emotional residue behind. Image-making is widely recognized to have physical, psychological and spiritual healing attributes that we can avail ourselves of.

Image-making can also enabling us to play and relax. The importance of playing, in the context of therapy, was highlighted by Winnicott (1974) who saw play and psychotherapy as intrinsically linked. He thought that therapists needed to facilitate clients' ability to play if that was an area of difficulty for them. For clinicians who work with children this is obvious, but perhaps less so for those who work with adult clients, and even less so when applied to ourselves. Play is an important part of our lives at all developmental stages, and it is a vital part of creativity. It can be fun and serious at the same time. In Winnicott's terms, it connects us to our vital sense of self and meaning. We can use art materials to play and we can gain great satisfaction and contentment from experimenting with different artistic media for fun.

Points for reflection

The challenge here is to create a self portrait – or rather a portrait of your various selves. It is an activity that can be as light hearted or as serious as you wish.

Think about the person you are now and your life at present, and gather together a selection of images from magazines or other, perhaps more personal sources such as photographs. You can use other materials such as fabrics, wool, wrapping paper, kitchen foil, packaging – anything readily available in your everyday life. Experiment!

When you have collected together your pictures find some drawing paper, preferably of about A3 size, some scissors and strong glue. Organize the image in whatever way seems to suit you, cutting and pasting your materials onto the paper. You might like to add text or to scribble over images with felt pens; play with the materials.

Only when you have finished your picture or collage, consider what it means for you and why you chose to depict the things you did. You might like to try a conversation with the different selves that you can recognize in the image. What do they say to you?

I would encourage you to give yourself personal time for creative play, which can provide insight, refreshment and pleasure. Making art impacts our senses on many levels, engaging our conscious and unconscious thought processes, our emotions, our senses and our bodily responses. Art provides us with a visual language which has the potential to transcend barriers of understanding and communication. There are many different mediums to work with, either within or outside artistic conventions such as perspective and representation. Artistic materials can produce wonderful colours, textures and shapes, and they can be manipulated in any way that we choose, pushing boundaries of discovery and opening up fascinating and absorbing avenues of interest. When we make art in whatever form, we engage with the possibility of working with the expanse of our imagination. The possibilities are boundless.

Further resources

Books on self-exploration through creativity:

Gaynor, S. (2009). *Creative Awakenings: Envisioning the Life of Your Dreams Through Art*. Cincinnati: North Light Books.
Ramsay, G. and Sweet, H. (2008). *A Creative Guide to Exploring Your Life. Self-Reflection Using Photography, Art and Writing*. London: Jessica Kingsley Publications.
Roberts, K.R. (2008). *Taking Flight: Inspiration and Techniques to Give Your Creative Spirit Wings*. Cincinnati: North Light Books.
Soneff, S. (2008). *Art Journals and Creative Healing: Restoring The Spirit Through Self-Expression*. Massachusetts: Quarry Books.

On art therapy:

Edwards, D. (2004). *Art Therapy*, London: Sage Publications.
McNiff, S. (2004). *Art Heals: How Creativity Cures the Soul*, Boston: Shambhala Publications Inc.
www.baat.org

On self-care:

Norcross, J.C. and Guy, J.D. (2007). *Leaving It At the Office. A Guide to Psychotherapist Self-Care*, New York: The Guilford Press.

8
Developing through Embodiment and Movement

Tom Warnecke

Self awareness and learning through others involve examining our ways of being in the world, the impact of personal and cultural experiences, our values and beliefs and our patterns of communication. All these dimensions of being invariably include bodily aspects – our self placement in the world is necessarily and irreducibly embodied. Paraphrasing Simone de Beauvoir (1989), our body is the primary instrument of our grasp upon the world.

Do I *have* a body or *am* I a body? This question may sound academic but serves to highlight the paradoxical nature of our relationship with our organism. Our relationship with our body is permeated by its associations with pleasure and performance, as a source of erotic desire and powerful passions, and the subject of fears, loathing or idealizations. It is shaped by our sensory experience of being a body, but also by our perceptions of our own physical appearance and our ideas about how others perceive us.

Do we usually look at our body from an externalized, third-person view, or perhaps more from an internalized, first-person experience? From a third-person perspective, we may see the body as an object or as a sexual image that solicits criticism, idealizations or fears. From a first-person perspective, my body is always *soma*, a living body, and experienced as an *I am*. A self-sensing perception of myself differs radically from any objectifying perception. My sense as a living body-self will, for example, incorporate some felt-sense awareness of my affect states, movement activity, visceral sensations and respiration. Most of us will do both, of course. Reviewing how we experience our body will nonetheless engage us with central aspects of our *identity*.

Significant characteristics of ourselves, such as age, height and weight, ethnicity, disabilities, gender or sexual orientation inform our sensory awareness of ourselves but also our perception of bodily appearance. Stereotypes of 'normality' and 'abnormality' or aesthetic ideals in our cultural and social worlds shape our experiences of living with body differences.

Consider the following questions:

Points for reflection

How do you usually relate to your body? In the first person or third person?

Can you identify the contexts in which you might choose one or the other?

Describe your body image of yourself. Are you comfortable with it?

How do you relate to other important bodily aspects of yourself?

Over the last two decades neuroscientists have focused their quest for the building blocks of human functioning on psycho-biological phenomena. This approach produced a wealth of new evidence, stimulated interdisciplinary dialogue on mind-brain-body relations and widened interest in psyche-soma theories. In his book *Descartes' Error*, the renowned neuroscientist Damasio (1994) took a resolutely anti-Cartesian stand. He argued that body states form the neural substrate of selfhood. Our bodily self experience provides indispensable references for subjective perception and the functions of the mind. Damasio described selfhood as a repeatedly reconstructed biological state, or in other words, the subliminal *'I am'* experience of the living body.

Sensory experience of the living body is essential for the development and continuity of selfhood. The social-relational narrative of identity becomes grounded in somato-sensory experience. We only truly appreciate this vital aspect when faced with its absence. Deficiencies of continuous self experience are a central feature of all severe psychopathologies. Even in mild or moderate distress, there will be some impairment of our sensory self awareness.

In this chapter, I will explore the body as an agency for self-discovery and learning and introduce some physiological aspects of mind-body relations to demystify and make psyche-soma dynamics accessible.

Bodily experience and the 'other'

Whenever two people meet there is a continuous exchange of signals that influences and modulates the bodily and psychological states of both participants. Two sensory-motor systems and two autonomic nervous systems become aware of each other and begin to respond, interact and relate in some way or form. Our limbic and motor nervous systems are designed to resonate, regulate, predict and respond.

Sally is at work. She feels calm and at ease today. Alice enters Sally's office visibly upset and in distress. Naturally, Sally is impacted by Alice's state but she is also able to retain a calm and composed state. She acknowledges her colleague's distress with empathy and enquires about what has upset Alice. It doesn't take long for Alice to feel comforted and tell Sally about her experience.

Now imagine a different narrative for this scenario: Sally does not retain her calm mind-body state but becomes anxious and agitated herself in response to Alice's distress. Most likely, Alice will not calm down and her distress may even increase as a result of their encounter.

Neuroscientists describe this process as co-regulation of psycho-biological events. As a species, we rely on co-regulation whenever the intensity of affect and emotional states exceeds or overwhelms our capacity to self-regulate. This equally applies to positive states. What do you do when you receive some fantastic news? Most likely you tell a friend and share your excitement.

The sensory-motor system's ability to feel movements, postures and emotional states observed in others is also referred to as kinesthetic resonance. In recent years, neuroscientists have identified a mirror neuron system. Mirror neurons activate neuronal motor representations whenever we observe the activities of others. For example, my sensori-motor cortex not only becomes active when I reach for an object but also when I watch someone else doing this. Mirroring is a pre-reflective, intuitive and spontaneous process closely associated with the sensory-motor system. Mirror neurons are part of an action resonance system designed to capture and understand the actions of others. This enables me not only to perceive and assess the intentions and actions of others but also to co-experience and feel empathy.

Our bodily structures and rhythms can only develop reciprocally with the rhythms and structures of our immediate environment. Any emerging sense of self is necessarily intersubjective as well as bodily subjective, derived from interactive experiences with important others. Early development depends crucially on mapping motor-sensory elements of body-to-body experiences in resonantly attuned relationships. Bodily and limbic resonance allows us to assimilate any self-regulatory functions and skills of others.

The ability to distinguish between self and non-self experiences is vital, however. Without some sufficiently functional self-other distinction, we would struggle to understand and engage with the intentions, beliefs and emotional states of others. Inferring the emotional expression of another requires me to compare my assessment of their emotional state with my own. My ability to distinguish and compare my emotional states with those of another forms the basis for empathic responses, helps me form perspectives and guides my actions.

Self regulation

While co-regulation relies on the regulatory support of the other, self regulation is largely facilitated by our sensory–motor skills. Sensory–motor activity, with support from respiratory and autonomic nervous systems, provides a container for affect states and our emotional experience.

Carl has been referred by his physiotherapist who treats his back at regular intervals. He is a tall, mixed race 28-year-old, whose stature and features display his father's West African heritage.

'My lower back is weak,' Carl explains. 'I'm ok right now. I do my physiotherapy exercises every morning. I end up in pain if I don't.'

Carl's physiotherapist encouraged him to address emotional issues and suggested somatic psychotherapy. Carl was injured in a car crash at the age of 9 and he is the only survivor of the accident, which killed both his father and his older brother.

I notice that I feel a bit unsettled, which makes me wonder about Carl. Is he is perhaps a little anxious beneath his outwardly calm manner? I decide to propose a bodily exercise and Carl agrees. He follows my demonstration of the position and we both sit on the floor with our backs to a wall and knees drawn up.

'Push against the wall with your back on your in-breath,' I instruct him, 'then stop pushing and relax your hips and pelvis as you breathe out.'

'Which part of my back should I push with?' he enquires.

'Whatever comes naturally,' I respond. 'But try pushing lighter and harder against the wall and see which feels best for you right now.'

Carl follows my suggestions and settles into a rhythm after a while.

'This is good,' he says a little later. 'I feel calmer now. I was a bit worried about coming here and talking to you.'

'How is your lower back?' I enquire.

'Pretty good,' Carl responds. 'I feel more solid there and stronger now.'

The calming effect of the exercise is achieved through motor mobilization in conjunction with sensory activity and respiration and it may provide support with anxieties, distress or even panic attacks. This exercise will only be effective if Carl uses his sensory awareness to identify his momentary preferences and adjusts his motor effort accordingly.

Our motor system's sensory capacity compels and informs the reciprocal relationship between psychological and bodily dimensions of self. Sensory representation systems are basic and yet vital elements of information processing. They shape our momentary subjective experience of ourselves and of the world around us and, in the process, underpin and organize cognitive functions. Body states are the bedrock of our sense of being alive. Sensations track and map the moment-to-moment landscapes of the body. The somatosensory system consists of sensory receptors and neural pathways that facilitate our experience of sensations arising from touch, pressure or temperature, but in particular, also from muscle movement and joint positions. Such sensory activities and awareness deteriorate rapidly in challenging situations when our focus shifts towards some perceived external threat.

'I've always avoided talking about the accident and my father's and brother's death,' Carl tells me a week later. 'I make a joke or change the subject when this comes up.'

Carl has few memories of the accident. He recalls waking up in hospital and the many weeks spent there in recovery. Carl appears calm but I appreciate the warning that this is a difficult subject for him. I suggest a breathing exercise to keep him anchored in his body.

During the exercise, Carl becomes aware of the area between his solar plexus and his navel. 'It's like a drum skin here,' he says and touches himself, 'hard, tight and bouncy.'

I observe a slight protrusion where his fingers indicate. Carl recalls being told about his father's and brother's death by his uncle.

'I was numb. I couldn't cry. And I felt really bad that I didn't cry.'

'My mother needed a lot of support and I tried to be strong for her and my little sister. I guess I wanted to become the man in the family.'

I suggest to Carl that he try to find a posture or movement that supports his lower back. He gets up from his chair and stretches in various ways.

'See if you find something that feels nice or pleasurable.' I want to invite and encourage new self-regulatory impulses in Carl's organism.

'I like the movement,' Carl replies. 'Can I lie down on the carpet?'

'Be my guest,' I respond.

Carl is lying on his back and continues to explore stretch positions before he eventually settles into quiet contemplation. After a while, his hands return to the midriff.

'It feels much softer now,' he tells me and he starts a gentle drumming motion with his hands as if to illustrate his sensory experience.

'How do you feel in your lower back?' I enquire.

'I feel warmth there.'

It seems that Carl relied too much on his lower back, midriff and diaphragm to compensate for the shock and emotional trauma of the accident.

Movements and postures form the body's primary language. Any sensory experience arising from posture, movement and facial expression is defined as proprioception or kinesthesia. Proprioception is seen as a distinct sensory modality that informs us whether our body is moving with required effort and where various parts of our body are located in space and in relation to each other. Muscles are sensory organs and our emotional self-experience depends crucially on the sensory information they facilitate. A feeling of heaviness in my chest originates from my respiratory muscles' subjective sense of effort. This effort may facilitate the extra oxygen required for some demanding physical activity or, equally, compensate for a contraction in my chest arising from a feeling of sadness.

In the early twentieth century, Wilhelm Reich discovered how respiration and motor activities regulate our emotional experience and expression. Physiological tensions evoked by stress or fear responses in motor and respiratory systems can bind and compensate anxiety, he observed. Repressed affect or emotional states and inhibited motor impulses may develop into chronic patterns of restrained respiration and bodily tension and become part of our learned physiological behaviour. This is known as 'muscular armour' and is used to defend against or protect feelings and vulnerabilities.

The sensory–motor system is also an agency for dissociative responses. Motor and sensory functions are split to numb and reduce the emotional intensity of trauma or make conflicts less overwhelming. Sensory cognition is facilitated by residual muscle tension or 'tone', a continuous and passive partial contraction of a muscle that indicates its readiness for action. It is achieved by the relative number of motor units activated and remains active even when the organism is resting. Both hypo- and hyper-distortions of tone can bind and compensate anxiety but this will invariably diminish the flow of sensory information.

Tone, and the readiness for action and motor confidence it manifests, determines the degree of autonomy and confidence we subconsciously experience, compels our mental perceptions and informs our belief systems about ourselves. At the other end of the scale, proprioceptive sensations of unbalanced or inadequate muscle tone are also known to fuel states of unspecified anxiety or nameless dread. Tone reflects and responds to interactions between my inner world and my external environment.

Psyche and soma as dimensions of self

In ancient Greece, the person was seen as a union of psyche and soma, in contrast to later Christian and Cartesian traditions, which split body and soul/self into polar opposites. Greek philosophers and poets initially used the word 'soma' for corpse and saw the body as an assemblage of individual organs rather than as a unit. By the early sixth century B.C., however, soma had become redefined as a living body and psyche as a soul or self inhabiting this living body but not associated with any of its organs.

The changing awareness of psyche and soma coincided with newfound appreciations of the agonies of erotic desire. The undeniable intensity of emotional bodily experience in passionate desire and unrequited love, it seems, compelled recognition of psyche as the body's inner dimension. Eros evokes bodily states of passion, anguish, confusion or helplessness, imbues music and poetry with expressions of sensuality, longing and consummation, individualizes our experience and awakens the body-mind to itself.

Like the ancient Greek before him, Reich observed the psycho-erotic build-up of physiological tension which formed the basis for his ground-breaking theories on character, muscular armour and sexuality. This understanding became the foundation for all body psychotherapy approaches and inspired interventions aimed at breaking through, or dissolving, restrictive muscular armour and unlocking the body's self-regulating potential. Eventually, researchers realized that a lack of protective psyche-motor skills was as undesirable as excessive armouring patterns. They found that psyche-motor skills constitute indispensable aspects of self and ego-functions. Theory and practice developed which recognize and utilize the dynamic 'self' organizing capacity of sensory-motor systems.

Winnicott, a contemporary of Reich, was drawn by yet another aspect of psyche-soma relations. He observed the vital importance of bodily experiences within resonant attachment relationships to achieve an adequate development of self. Winnicott's conceptualized 'true self' is an embodied self that maintains a continuity of being through sensory cognition. His notion of 'psyche dwelling in soma' expanded the Greek paradigm and emerged as a frame to think about and explore mind-body dichotomy and interconnectedness as determining factors to the multidimensional nature of the self. The lodgement of psyche in soma, Winnicott concluded, constitutes a central and indeed indispensable aspect of 'self' development.

The infant's earliest intra-psychic and interpersonal experiences are bodily-felt phenomena. Movement and sensory stimuli help the infant to organize experiences of self and other. In the words of the renowned body-mind researcher Deane Juhan, 'by rubbing up against the world, I define myself to myself' (1987: 34). Many aspects of such bodily self awareness will only be felt in the subliminal realm of the sensory-motor cortex. Nonetheless, sensory cognition and awareness of the living body enable us to contain and organize the intrapsychic space of our psychological self. Motor and sensory cognition skills provide the building blocks for our organism's capacities to dynamically 'self' organize.

Carl tells me a week later that he stayed in touch with his midriff since our last session. 'It varies,' he says, 'but it has been softer on a number of occasions.'

After a repeat of the breathing exercise, I suggest to Carl to close his eyes and imagine watching the accident from a bird's eye perspective. Carl makes himself comfortable and begins to describe the scenery as the images arise in his mind. This process does not appear to trigger stress responses from his autonomic nervous system. On the contrary, I observe Carl's out-breath deepening after a while.

'I can sense a space in front of my belly where the hard bounciness was,' Carl interrupts himself a little later. His hands indicate the region between his solar plexus and his navel, an area often associated with fear states. 'There is air now and I'm breathing there,' Carl explains.

'I feel I've been uprooted by the accident.'

Carl has a wide circle of friends but also keeps everybody at a distance, he says. There is no shortage of female lovers in his life, occasionally more than one, but only for short periods of time. He never attempted a relationship with a girlfriend, Carl tells me apologetically.

Sensory–motor and autonomic nervous systems learn from pleasure as well as from pain and contribute crucially to our continuous self-sense and well-being. We may feel numb, depressed or flooded by waves of inexplicable emotional states when the steady stream of consciousness arising from moment-to-moment somato–sensory information is stunted or absent. Accidents and other traumatic events may affect all aspects of a person but particularly disrupt their bodily self experience and psyche – soma integration. Hermann (1992) described how linguistic encoding of memory becomes inactivated in states of high sympathetic arousal and our nervous systems revert to sensory forms of memory which predominate in early life.

Trauma and shock are emotional and sensory experiences and many people struggle to reconstruct a cognitive narrative of their experience. In the aftermath of challenging or traumatic events, psyche and soma aspects of self commonly need to be restored to one another to revive body and mind from numbness, immobility or hyper-arousal. The somatic trauma work approach developed by Merete Holm Brantbjerg (2007) utilizes psyche-motor skills to restore sensory-motor integration, re-balance the autonomic nervous system and put disjointed sensations together instead of fostering cathartic re-experience of a traumatic event.

Carl's physique displays his passion for sport. My aim is to utilise Carl's well-developed motor skills as a basis from which to further expand his awareness into psyche-soma dialogue and integration.

'I want you to push the floor down with your right foot,' I instruct Carl.

We are both standing and he looks at me questioningly. 'Are you serious?'

'Use your leg muscles to push against the floor,' I repeat my invitation and model the movement for him.

'Now shift to your left leg and push with your left foot,' I continue a little while later.

'And back to your right foot.'

'Keep alternating, pushing the floor down with your left and right foot.'

'My right leg feels strong but it's very different in my left leg,' he responds.

'I feel weak on my left side and I don't want to push down.'

'My right foot is solid on the ground but I don't feel much contact from my left foot to the floor.'

Carl's left leg is awakening to its own agenda. it appears. He attempts to assert his will but the confounding motor intentions become increasingly visible in Carl's slow movements.

'My left foot seems to want to move up instead of down,' Carl comments on his internal struggle.

'It's such a contrast to my right foot. I feel really solid there and it's almost as if the floor is lifting me up when I push down.'

I contemplate Carl's struggle by sensing my own leg movements before encouraging him to pursue his involuntary motor intentions.

'I'd like you to experiment a bit and see where your left leg wants to go.'

Carl seems to hesitate and I repeat my invitation.

'Just allow and follow these upward movements in your left leg and foot.'

Carl ponders this as he continues to shift between his right and left legs. I watch his inner struggle and observe the initial attempts to accommodate this impulse. The upward lift in his left leg is tentative at first but gathers momentum and becomes increasingly self-assured with each repetition. Carl continues to shift between his right and left legs but these movements now combine an upward lift on his left with a downward push on his right. To a casual observer, this may look very similar to his earlier movements but Carl is enthralled by his discovery.

'I feel less weak now in my left side,' he proclaims. 'This is amazing.'

His movements become increasingly fluid and are accompanied by facial expressions that convey relaxation and make him appear younger. Carl later tells me that his left leg had been injured in the crash.

Movements serve to intensify our sensory perception and to help us to inhabit our momentary experience. The perceptual–sensual awakening potential of movement and the depth and intensity of insight it affords is well established and utilized by many dance, movement and body psychotherapies. Movements and gestures contain symbolic functions and serve to bridge fragmented aspects of ourselves. Emotions are body states: they are complex psycho–physiological events that combine mental, visual, auditory and sensory perception with respiratory, visceral and motor responses.

Emotional body states are triggered by external or internal stimuli (a recollection of a previous event for instance) and may utilize any aspect of our organism. A gut feeling, or gut reaction, is a visceral emotional response. Emotions help us to organize our responses to our environment, to assess situations and how we relate to them in the context of our internal experience.

'I've been quite aware of my left side for a few days. I also made contact with my uncle,' Carl reports when we meet again.

'He's my father's brother and I only see him rarely. I called him and he has invited me to come up and stay with him and his family next weekend. I want to talk to him about my father.'

Carl, divorced from his body in the aftermath of the accident, apparently also enacted his internal alienation in his external environment and relationships with others by avoiding close family bonds as well as romantic involvement.

I suggest we return to last week's exercise and Carl readily agrees.

'Push down against the floor with your right leg,' I instruct.

'Now shift to your left side and feel where your leg wants to go today.'

'I feel like pushing down a bit actually,' Carl responds after some reflection.

'I'm pushing more gently than on my right side but it feels ok today.'

Carl appears to settle into an increasingly effortless rhythm.

'Now I want you to become aware of your out-breath,' I suggest a little later.

'Imagine a parachute landing on the ground. Picture how the parachute looses its shape and gently deflates as it lands.'

'Allow your upper body to deflate like the parachute as you breathe out.'

Carl's movements between left and right increase in fluidity and I repeat my instructions.

I observe his spine and shoulders moving with each out-breath. 'Allow your shoulders to participate in your movements,' I encourage him.

He continues to shift from one leg to the other and his movements increasingly assume a dance-like quality.

After some 15 minutes, Carl yawns. 'I'm sorry,' he apologizes and yawns again. 'I must be more tired than I thought.'

'I can feel both my legs more now,' Carl tells me, 'and my vision is clearer.'

'I see objects more sharply.'

Carl's yawning signals an autonomic nervous system shift from sympathetic to parasympathetic arousal. Sympathetic arousal is known as 'fight-flight' response as opposed to restorative and integrative functions of parasympathetic activity. Our perception and cognition are powerfully influenced by the regulatory capacities of both branches.

Any significant arousal of the sympathetic branch will invariably diminish my sensory cognition and affect my thinking to turn increasingly towards 'either-or' perspectives. As my organism becomes more and more governed by fight-flight responses, my perception will follow suit and increasingly view any given situation in survival mode. When my organism subsequently lands in the parasympathetic realm, my mental process will simultaneously move from 'either-or' back towards pluralistic 'both-and' perspectives, which allows me to digest and integrate my experience.

Stanley Keleman coined the phrase 'your body speaks its mind' (1989) but we could just as validly say 'our mind speaks its body'. Strictly speaking, any state of mind constitutes a psycho-physiological event that incorporates specific experiences such as degree of relaxation and anxiety, alertness, calmness and agitation, or, in a depression, low sensory-motor arousal.

Carl is excited that the weekend with his uncle went well.

'I had a fantastic time,' he tells me. 'It's great to be back in touch with my family and I want to see them more often.'

Carl wants to talk about his career. He is considering pursuing a PhD in his field. 'My father was an academic and I would want him to be proud of me.'

Carl enjoys his current university research post but is unsure if he wants to pursue this as a career.

'Do you think I should follow into my father's footsteps?' Carl asks me a short while later.

Our relationship seems to move into parental terrain. As I contemplate my response, I become aware that my sensory self experience is rapidly diminishing. I also notice a feeling of not wanting to disappoint Carl. My sense of disembodiment appears relevant to Carl's process and I decide to explore his question with movement. Carl begins to stretch and move about as soon as he gets up. I follow suit and notice a revival of my sensory cognition.

There are several carpets on the floor and we designate one as the academic career path he associates with his father. I invite Carl to step into this space. After preparing himself mentally, Carl steps forward.

'Whoa, I'm not sure if like this.'

'I don't want to turn into my father.'

'Step back into your earlier position,' I suggest as a way of exploring Carl's feelings.

'Is there anything happening for you now?' I ask Carl as he looks at the space he just occupied.

'I feel a bit angry actually,' Carl replies.

'About anything in particular?' I ask.

Carl is unsure at first but he is able to clarify his feelings after stepping once more onto the other carpet.

'I feel let down by my father. I know it's unfair to say this but he wasn't there when I needed him most.'

Movements serve to intensify our sensory perception and cognition and allow us to inhabit our momentary experience. Hidden inner conflicts or internalized others become amplified and more accessible when we bodily occupy a symbolizing object space. We can also explore these through movements. Moving between symbolizing objects may facilitate dialogue between internal characters. Similar techniques can engage with body organs or limbs if they symbolize internal characters in conflict, through ill-health, for instance.

Episodes of trauma activation or hidden internal conflicts can bodily affect others present. In my psychotherapeutic work, I regularly observe fluctuations of my sensory cognition and self-experience. My awareness of embodiment and disembodiment phenomena adds texture and depth to the therapeutic working alliance and it can provide important clues about hidden conflicts or relational tensions.

Carl arrives in a state of agitation. He had a confrontation with another car driver. His agitation serves to heighten my awareness of his powerful physique and I allow myself to be impacted by his blackness. I do not feel threatened in any way but I notice the potential for such feelings in myself. I am aware that we have not had an opportunity to talk about our ethnic difference and, after some consideration, I decide to broach the subject.

'How do feel talking to a white man about your life?'

'I don't know. I don't think colour is all that important.'

'It may not be important but it may be relevant in some way or form,' I respond. 'The colour of our skins is a reality and I imagine you have some feelings about it.'

'I wonder if this man in the car park would have behaved in the same way if I didn't look black,' Carl warms to the subject.

'I am quite angry with black men for behaving stupidly and making my life difficult with their behaviour. I am also angry with white people,' Carl's voice is rising with agitation.

'They don't see me. They just react to the black man they see. White people don't understand what it's like.'

Carl keeps looking at me as if he is unsure about my response. 'I don't mean you', he seeks to reassure me, 'but people in general.'

I feel calm and alert and encourage him with a nod to continue. Carl smiles. His posture and breathing suggest that he is comfortable; our working alliance appears solid enough to explore these uncharted waters.

'I'm confused. I don't quite understand where I fit in. My parent's families are so different and I don't know where I belong.' He ponders this for a while before getting deeper into the subject.

'When my father was alive we lived in a village. People were friendly but the colour of my skin was never mentioned. Maybe it made them uneasy and they avoided it?'

'This all changed when we moved to London after the accident. I was called names and heard racist remarks. Later, when I was 13 or 14, I was quite big for my age and some people were afraid of me, in the shops for example. They thought I would rob their store or something. It made me angry to see their

fear. Why did they have to be afraid of me? I was just a kid. Sometimes it made me want to do something – just to show them – is this what you want from me? But I didn't do it of course.'

'I've never talked about this to anybody. But it's good to be able to say these things to you.'

Carl's experience is not uncommon. Visible features of cultural or ethnic difference, which could provide essential points of references to construct identity, often remain paradoxically unnamed and unacknowledged in our society. They nonetheless signal status or class of the individual, suggest trustworthiness or potential threats to others, or they may get used for derogative or abusive attacks by others.

Some existential meaning of ethnic or cultural differences and similarities may thus stay unavailable to support self-acceptance and shape individual identity. To individuals of minority heritage, who already struggle to construct their identity in what may well appear an ocean of otherness, such apparent invisibility may seem an outright denial of their identity.

Intersubjective theory postulates that we must be recognized by the other as another subject to fully experience and establish our subjective selfhood in the other's presence (Benjamin 1990). This need for recognition, Benjamin suggests, cannot be fulfilled without a capacity to recognize others in return and, by extension, achieve some mutual recognition. In an inter-cultural context, such mutual recognition must necessarily include any significant aspects of embodied identity, be they colour, race, gender, class, disability or sexual orientation. A shared experience of difference in the therapeutic relationship may essentially deepen both inter- and intra-psychic experiences for client and therapist (Ablack 2008).

This could also apply to other, less visible aspects of bodily differences. Posture and movement patterns may embody cultural context and subtly communicate sameness and difference. The rhythms, patterns and waves of body language constitute vital forms of communication and include facial expressions, how close we stand, how much eye contact we make and the tone of our voices. Meaning and interpretations of bodily expressions are not universally recognized but are defined by cultural and individual contexts. A posture of arms folded in front of the body for instance, is viewed as a gesture of respect for the other person in some parts of Africa. In Europe, this same posture would be commonly seen as closed or defensive towards others.

We generally aim to establish rapport by matching the speech patterns and bodily rhythms of others. Similarities in posture, gestures and tone of voice signal understanding and approval. During childhood, we learn how to modulate our movements and our patterns and tone of speech to be in tune with others and to initiate, regulate or terminate social interaction. Such abilities to communicate non-verbally are indispensable to establish relationships successfully. We all notice when somebody's voice is too loud for the occasion. People with Asperger syndrome often experience themselves 'out of sync' with others, for example. They struggle to match the non-verbal behaviour of others who in turn may perceive their mode of communication as challenging.

Many of our postures and gestures originate from adaptations to inner or outer pressures we experienced at that time. They may incorporate chronic tensions or aches but they could also embody particular belief systems or some introjected aspect of a significant other. Movements and postures are learned and the sensory qualities of newfound movements can help us establish new ways of being. Movements may also deepen and elucidate a feeling and connect us to its context.

Carl has spent more time with members of his father's family. He is also keen to see more of his current girlfriend and seems to become more attached to the relationship.

'I never realised how much I had isolated myself,' he tells me. 'It makes me sad.'

'I feel a bit heavy in my heart.'

I suggest he finds a movement with one or both hands that matches his feeling. He leans forward in his chair and his hands move toward his back. Soon both hands, palms facing outward, are moving gently up and down his lower back. I invite Carl to extend the movement and allow other parts of his body to participate in some way. A short while later Carl stands up. His arms spread out and move like wings.

'Is there perhaps an image that connects to both your feeling and your movement?' I enquire.

'I see a cage,' Carl says. 'I've been in it and I want out.'

Self awareness – an embodied perspective

We speak with our bodies and our bodies resonate with the presence, actions and expressions of others. Our internal modes of communication are not limited to intrapsychic voices or configurations only. Some internal characters manifest as felt-sense experience within the organism. The intricacies of psyche–soma dynamics provide us with a vast range of 'self' referencing frames. You could ask yourself the following questions in any given situation:

Points for reflection

What is my internal response to this situation?
  Can I feel my whole body?
  Is my breath calm and steady? Do I struggle to breathe or hold my breath?
  Can I feel my feet on the ground? Are they warm or cold?
  Do I feel heavy or light in my body? Am I warm and animated or perhaps stiff and frozen?
  What happens to my bodily self experience when I now move?

Observing such sensory and often subliminal experience is an integral aspect of self reflection and, crucially, facilitates psyche–soma communication when faced with difficult situations. Any situation we experience as challenging will impact us and may profoundly affect our self functions. Sensations associated with anxiety or fear states are not pleasant and we may seek to avoid them. Unfortunately this comes at a price. We sacrifice sensory cognition, our principal facility to negotiate the dynamic tensions of mind–body relations.

Learning through embodiment and movement begins with awareness of my own bodily experience. Through sensory awareness, I can integrate self experience with self expression. I may, for example, sense my exhilaration or the flow of my movements as I dance, feel my breath while I speak or my feet on the ground as I walk. Awareness of embodiment and movement forges a path towards authenticity, individuation, self awakening and self recognition, facilitates my recognition of others and my mutual relationships with them.

Perceiving through the body and its felt senses also deepens my ability to engage with intimacy and interrelatedness in relationships while at the same time maintaining my self experience. I observe the internal adaptations in myself and in the other and yield to the symphonies of our mutual exchange.

Further resources

Body psychotherapy:

Contemporary Body Psychotherapy: The Chiron Approach, Ed. Hartley. (2008). Abingdon: Routledge.

Stauffer, K. (2010). *Anatomy & Physiology for Psychotherapists: Connecting Body & Soul*. New York: W.W. Norton & Co.

European Association for Body Psychotherapy: http://www.eabp.org/

United States Association for Body Psychotherapy: http://www.usabp.org/

Neuroscience:

Lewis T., Amini F., and Lannon R. (2000). *A General Theory of Love*. New York: Vintage Books.

Dance Movement Work:

Hartley, L. (1995). *Wisdom of the Body Moving: An Introduction to Body-Mind Centering*. Berkeley: North Atlantic Books.

Association for Dance Movement Therapy, U.K.: http://www.admt.org.uk/

American Dance Therapy Association: http://www.adta.org/

5 Rythms Dance information: http://en.wikipedia.org/wiki/5Rhythms

9
Developing through the Natural Environment

Tim Bray

This chapter takes the form of an interview, in which Tim Bray explores his own relationship with the natural environment in conversation with Chris Rose, the editor of this book. Although the questions asked are specifically about Tim, they also provide a template for the readers' exploration of their own relationship to the environment.

CR: *Would you say your relationship with the natural environment was a significant one?*

TB: My relationship with the natural environment has been significant and central throughout my life. It has been a source of comfort, of wonder and of challenge. I seem to have a deep need to immerse myself in the natural environment regularly and it gives me the greatest and simplest of pleasures. It offers an alternative to the materialist, consumer existence that most of us live in most of the time, and reminds me of what truly sustains us all. We are dependent on the natural environment for the basic things in life….. food, water, light… …and it seems to offer us opportunities to connect with it, with ourselves and with others.

Like many of us, I am very concerned at the impact human development, economic growth and population growth are having on the natural environment. The increasing concerns about climate change, the loss of habitat and ongoing environmental degradation all suggest a catastrophic and possibly irreversible change in our relationship with the natural environment. I don't want to be a harbinger of gloom, and there are signs that we are waking up to the enormity of the problem that the environment faces, but things don't look good. What it generates in me is a gnawing feeling of anxiety, a great sadness at our capacity to damage what is precious and feelings of helplessness about how to stop it. I know these feelings are shared by many with similar concerns.

We have the capacity to put our short-term desire for instant gratification above the need for living with awareness, of recognizing that our actions have consequences in the long-term for which we are responsible.

CR: *How do you think your early experiences might have influenced your relationship with the natural environment?*

TB: My mother grew up on a farm in Kent, the eldest of five children of farmers who moved up from Cornwall in the 1930s. I think it was a hard life. Her father and his two brothers left Cornwall and bought farms in Kent. My grandfather was the least successful of the three and eventually went bankrupt and lost the farm. He ended up working for the Milk Marketing Board. My mother trained and worked as a nurse in the local hospital in Tunbridge Wells. She had a connection with the land and an awareness of food and where it had come from. She valued the natural environment and embarrassed me as a child by picking up litter as she walked me to school in the village. I find myself doing the same thing now and embarrassing my own children!

My mother died twenty years ago and two memories of her come back strongly. The first is of us sitting together in the garden, me aged about six, podding broad beans for supper; the quiet satisfying labour of preparing food together, the gentle talk of mother and child. Secondly, I remember at a similar age snoozing after lunch in a hammock with her, hung beneath the shade of an old hawthorn tree on a hot summer's day. I still have the hammock, bought in Brazil 50 years ago, where I was born.

My father was from Lincolnshire, the grandson of fishermen and coopers, working out of the docks in Grimsby. My grandfather worked in an ironmonger's in Boston until his retirement and then ran the shop at Butlins in Skegness. For him, the garden in his small bungalow was his piece of heaven, with immaculate rows of vegetables and flowers, and prizes won in the local gardening shows. My father, as part of the post-war generation with a grammar school education, broke away from his roots, moved to London and ended up working in the Foreign Office, living abroad for most of his career. His connection with the natural environment was expressed both through his passion for his garden and vegetable garden (like his father), but also through a more scientific interest in ferns and fungi. He has been a member of local groups monitoring and recording these plants for many years. This latter interest seems to combine a fascination with the variety and beauty of the plants, pleasure derived from the search for and finding of rare species, a desire to list and categorize, and the intellectual challenge of time spent with more formally trained colleagues.

What I learnt from my parents was that the natural environment was something to be valued and protected. Also that active engagement, in particular growing things, was something that could provide pleasure, and that waiting for things, delayed gratification, could be immensely satisfying. The planting of the seed, nurturing the seedling, harvesting and eating the crop and the saving of seed for next year were all part of the wonderful cycle of life.

They also taught me that nature was for 'being in' rather than 'doing in'. To sit quietly, by myself or with another, could be a calming, soothing experience and one I was to draw on deeply in later years.

CR: *That sounds as if you have found something nurturing in the natural environment?*

TB: The natural environment became a resource that I drew on deeply throughout my childhood, and continue to now. My childhood was disrupted by the experience of being sent to boarding school at the age of eight. My father was posted to Taiwan in 1965 and I went to boarding school with my two older brothers. I was terrified by the separation and spent time alternatively distressed or 'frozen'. I didn't see my parents for about three months, then [I went] to Taiwan for Christmas for three weeks, then back to school until the summer holidays in July; a gap of six to seven months. Easter holidays were spent at a 'holiday home' for boys in a similar position. My relationship with my parents, and my mother in particular, went from close attachment to wary distrust and confusion. None of this was spoken about or made sense of by the adults around me.

Beneath my cheerful, team playing, 'everything's fine' exterior lay anxiety, fear, sadness and social withdrawal. I battled with these feelings for many, many years. As with many of my contemporaries, I looked for relief by using alcohol, drugs, sex and risk-taking activities either to anaesthetize myself or to feel more alive. But there was another resource, that of the natural environment, that provided solace and comfort; a place where I could find out more about myself and others– a place where I could rest.

Paradoxically it was at school that I first became aware of nature as a place of nurturing and healing. I spent many hours alone and with friends hiding in the large rhododendron plantations in the school grounds. As a skinny boy I could climb into the foliage, twenty or thirty feet off the ground and disappear into the canopy. The other place to disappear was by the large lake where we were allowed to go fishing. Again many hours were spent on warm summer days drowsily watching the fishing float, taking time out from the suffocating world of the school a few hundred yards away. The third encounter with the natural environment at school was through the camp, either officially through the scout troop, or unofficially through the secret places that small groups of boys would seek out to create space away from mainstream life – a place to retreat to where one didn't need to be on guard all the time, a place to be oneself, a place to create an identity separate from the oppressive hierarchy of the school.

CR: *Sometimes the natural environment is not just nurturing but also challenging. Was this part of its attraction?*

TB: Definitely! How high could I climb in the tree, could I jump from one branch to another, could we go out into the night scaring ourselves and being scared by the night sounds, the fear of being caught....a delicious and addictive excitement. This continued into adult life! At my secondary school, another boarding school, we had a Cadet Force that you had to join. Thankfully it had a small group for those interested in rock-climbing and other outdoor activities. By this time, at the age of 15, I had dropped out of all competitive and team sports and was seriously experimenting with drugs and alcohol. The school and the culture at the time were riddled with it and several friends became casualties, physically or psychologically. I think it was my involvement in the Outdoor Activities group that saved me. It channelled my need to take risks and challenged me in a positive way, opening the door to a new and limitless world...the mountains....the rivers......wilderness. I have been exploring that world ever since. I cherish opportunities to reconnect with a simpler, earthier life. I love the elemental connection between my body and the ground, when high on a mountain, or between me and water when canoeing down some wild river in Wales or Scotland. I love the connection between me and friends in that environment; a playfulness and a connection develops that doesn't need to be talked about.

CR: *There are two types of connections you talk about here that I would like to explore. One is about relationships with other people, that you mention often. It makes me wonder how far the natural environment is a container for human relationships, and how the same environment would be experienced without other people.*

TB: While I have done a lot of walking on my own in the mountains, a lot of the most powerful experiences have been 'with others nearby'. When mountaineering or rock climbing one is connected to 'the other' by 50 metres of thin nylon rope, aware of their presence, hoping they are paying attention to your struggle at the other end, hoping they will hold you if you fall, perhaps like the parent watching the child in the playground. But at the same time I am engaged in a very private struggle to solve the problem in front of me. Can I work out the moves required to get to the ledge above, do I have the physical strength and do I dare try? Often the lead climber can be out of sight around a corner trying to work out what to do next, very much on their own in the moment, the leader's partner sitting quietly on a ledge just feeling the occasional twitch on the rope and wondering if the leader is making progress. It can feel very lonely but exquisitely charged.

The incident described took place 25 years ago in Scotland. I was with two friends who had climbed and walked together for many years. We had been scrambling up an easy but very isolated ridge, Angels Ridge, that leads up to Angels Peak (aptly named), Sgur an Lochan Uiane. As we approached the summit after two hours of hard slog through thick snow and a complex route, we found ourselves in increasingly thickening cloud and strong winds, blowing fine spindrift into our faces. We were walking into what is known as a 'white-out', with deep snow on the ground and thick cloud causing disorientation and visibility down to a few feet. You lose the capacity to distinguish whether the ground is going up hill or down and distances become distorted.

We had to walk across the summit plateau area, knowing there was a drop of hundreds of feet into the corrie on our left but we couldn't see it. We knew the edge of the corrie can have a large cornice, an overhang of windblown snow, which is easy to fall through. We agreed to rope together and navigate carefully across the plateau to the opposite ridge to descend. The person in the lead was walking on a compass bearing and counting their

footsteps, the two behind checking the bearing and staying prepared to halt the leader's fall with the rope.

As you can imagine, senses were on full alert, with an element
of fear but also the confidence of having been in situations like
this before and knowing we had the skills and equipment to
keep safe. I entered a state of deep satisfaction, almost bliss, as we
moved carefully across the blasted plateau, warm inside my well-
insulated winter clothes, in touch with my companions through
the rope that linked us, but unable to see or talk to them, and
revelling in the extreme weather. This blissful experience was
further heightened as we slowly began to descend and dropped
below the cloud cover on the lee side of the mountain. The sun
broke through, lighting the snow flakes that continued to spin
around us. We all had big grins on our faces as we quietly came
down the mountain knowing we had shared one of those intense
mountain experiences that are never forgotten.

In terms of the self, these experiences leave me with a real
sense of connection, a 'touching-base' with who I really am
through my connection or experience of the natural environment. It reminds me that I am 'OK', that I have something to
offer others and that I don't have to be anyone else than who
I am. It is why I return again and again to such places, to strip
away all the 'stuff' that complicates my life, and allows me to
experience the simple elemental things. I find it interesting
that sharing the experience with others is also important. I had
thought that it was more of a solitary activity but, on reflection,
it seems to have created a reference point or connection that is
built on over the years with others. It tends to be an implicit
rather explicit connection, not spoken of in any depth, but it is
there nonetheless.

CR: *What about those times when you have been completely alone, without any human companionship?*

TB: I have mentioned times, particularly my early adulthood, when
I have been heavily burdened by feelings of anxiety. Finding
relationships and intimacy difficult if not impossible, I would at
times have gone away for a few days on my own. I spent a memorable week on Skye, walking, camping or staying in a remote
bothy that is open for walkers. Memories of this time centre on
quiet hours walking on empty beaches with only seals, otters and
the seabirds for company, and the spectacular Cuillin hills in the
background.

I thought that by going away on my own I could sort out the internal conflicts that raged within, of which I was partially aware. Of course I couldn't, but at least I got some respite and a chance to reconnect with the benign peaceful parts of the natural environment. It enabled me to 'recharge my batteries' and return home better able to face the challenges ahead. These events all occurred before my introduction to counselling or psychotherapy, and before I had begun to develop an emotional language through which I could describe and attempt to make sense of my life experience, either to myself or to others. I think of my drive to seek out these experiences as an unconscious attempt by the 'self' to move towards health and integration, but without the necessary insight or the capacity to 'think about' it psychologically that was required to manage it.

CR: *Some of the incidents you talk about sound frightening to me, but perhaps fear itself is an important element in the relationship with the natural environment?*

TB: As you suggest, the role of fear seems an important part of my relationship with the natural environment. My thinking about this now, in terms of my own personal journey, is that this environment provided me with a space in which I could 'play' with or explore my own feelings of fear and powerlessness. I was an anxious child, with justifiable feelings of abandonment and loss, away at an emotionally cold and loveless school, or at home where nothing was talked about and feelings could not be acknowledged. I was a fragile child looking for a way of developing and becoming a secure, confident adult without much, if any, guidance from caring adults.

I needed something to help me feel good about myself, and to compensate for or soothe the ever-present anxiety; struggling in the natural environment, whether on a cliff somewhere or just walking up in the mountains, seemed to provide just that.

The experience of physical pain seems to be a part of this too. There seems to be a perverse satisfaction in needing to scrape one's knuckles or knees repeatedly, to end the day with aching limbs to achieve the objective. It is as if I could only be allowed to rest after a great struggle. So the object might appear to be the top of the mountain or the cliff, but actually it seems to be as much about reaching an inner place of peace, where enough has been done and it is now alright to rest.

I realized over time that the activities that generated these feelings of excitement, self-worth, satisfaction and finally peace were somewhat illusory, certainly transitory and had an addictive quality. They had to be repeated constantly to maintain the 'positive' feelings; another mountain to climb, another risk to take, another thing on the list to be ticked off so that at the end of the day I could sit back and say I'm still all right. I began to see this driven quality not just in myself but also in those around me. In essence I began to see it all as a huge compensation for much deeper feelings of loss and grief.

I realized that being a good climber or an adventurous mountaineer was not enough. It didn't actually prepare me for the real 'hard work' of human living, how to relate to another, how to be a parent and how to relate to myself. The qualities of bravery, endurance and patience that I thought were being developed through my relationship with the natural environment were often lacking in my personal relationships. The anxiety and fear that had been ever present were still there at home and at work, waiting to get me. Hence the journey into counselling and psychotherapy, in reality a much more frightening adventure, but which offered me a real opportunity for understanding myself, and myself in relation to others.

I still go to the mountains, still rock climb, still search for the wilderness experiences but because I want to, not because I have to. I have a more playful attitude to it all and I don't need to show off any more. I love the feeling of competence and confidence I have when I am in the natural environment. I love the humility it evokes in me and the reminder that I and the rest of the human race are deeply connected with nature, if only we would realize it.

CR: *The other important connection that you talked about earlier was that of an elemental link between body and ground. Can you say more about this?*

TB: Reflecting on my 53 years of engaging with the natural environment I can see that it has provided me with a space where I can connect with the natural world, rather than the human constructed world. It can be uncomfortable, cold, wet, frightening. It can also be warm, nurturing and benign. It doesn't do what I want it to do but within that there is a reality and a liberation, which is a comfort. The mountains will not change; they have always been there, they will be there after I am gone and after we have all gone.

By allowing myself to experience this link between body and ground, or body and natural environment, I open myself to my place in the bigger picture. It seems important to remind myself regularly that I do exist in relationship to the natural world, that it is not something to run or hide from but rather a relationship to embrace and learn from. It is only by doing that that I– that all of us– will be able to develop a rational and sustainable relationship with the natural environment.

CR: *I want to ask you more about your own sense of self in relation to the natural environment. It sounds as if at times you are intensely aware of yourself and others, but some experiences seem to be more like losing the self. Can you say more about this aspect?*

TB: We live on the side of a hill in deep rural Herefordshire, down a quiet lane with little traffic or background human activity. The house is on the edge of a wood, which rises above the house like a great wave. At times it feels like the wood is going collapse on top of us, at other times it seems to protect us from the prevailing winds. In the distance we can see the long blue ridges of the Black Mountains, leading up to the sudden drop at Hay Bluff. Below the house lie two small fields of old established pastures that, at this time of year, are ablaze with dandelions and cowslips and many other flowers. On this first hot day in May, dandelion seeds drift lazily up through the garden, landing on the keyboard of the laptop as I labour with this piece of writing.

In the early evening, when all the jobs are done, I often find myself just sitting quietly somewhere outside, the house surrounded by singing birds and the bees still working on the comfrey bed, a vague awareness of domestic murmurings from the house and the land around falling into the dimming light. At moments like this I can experience a loss of self or a blending of myself and the whole. These moments can be quite transitory and need to be noticed. I find it easy to be distracted or too busy, the mind preoccupied with what has happened or what will happen tomorrow.

I walked with the dog the other evening through the neighbours' fields, below the house, and one of those blissful transcendent moments occurred. A sense of the urgency of spring abounds, with the first flush of new growth in the hedges, a cuckoo calling from the copse in the distance and an expectant stillness in the air. Suddenly it's as if I'm out of my body…. The pain of recent weeks has gone … …. I feel light and blissful…. I smile and call the dog and turn for home. These moments can't be planned for, just noticed and enjoyed.

CR: *You mention the dog. What part do animals play in your relationship with the natural world?*

TB: Animals obviously form part of the richly interconnected eco-system that make up the natural environment. In some ways the domesticated dog or cat, of which we have both in our family, remind us of our relationship with the environment. When the cat drags in another creature from the garden and eats it under the table, or the dog sets off after a rabbit when out in the woods it reminds me that we are all part of nature, 'red in tooth and claw' with animal instincts and drives.

Where we live we also come into contact with wilder animals. Birds are happy to share the bird table. Great tits, blue tits, wood-peckers, nuthatches, blackbirds all visit for the nuts and food scraps we put out. Some, like the robin, follow me round the gar-den, looking for food as the soil is turned and insects exposed. Others, like the family of buzzards living high in the trees across the valley, make us aware of their presence by their high whis-tling calls and effortless soaring on the wind.

Bats live in the attic of our house and on warm summer nights a walk up the lane in the evening will always be accompanied by their flitting flight, as they patrol the hedge lines, looking for moths and flies.

Frogs and toads colonize the garden and greenhouse, keeping the slugs and snails at bay. I love the toad's stony presence, as well as its leathery dry skin and ancient look. I mourn their loss in spring, when on one of those first milder and wetter nights they decide it is time to rise from their winter slumbers, deep in leaf mould in the woods, and find a mate. This involves crossing the lane, and by the end of the week the bodies of those that didn't make it lie flattened on the tarmac.

It is clear that animals are important to me, and I have a real sense from where I live that we share our living space with a whole community of creatures, insects, reptiles, birds and mam-mals. These are less able or not able at all to manipulate their environment in the way that human beings are able to do. Rather they are increasingly dependent on us to maintain and conserve habitats, and I can do that locally, in my own patch by garden-ing in an aware way and on a broader scale, by contributing to national campaigns.

Wild animals do fill me with a sense of wonder and make me realize that my occasional forays into the wilderness, living rough,

and living simply are in some way an attempt to get in touch with
what wild animals do and what our ancient ancestors did ... ... living in relationship with the natural environment rather than cutting myself off from it.

CR: *Collecting and classifying seems such a big part of many people's
interaction with the natural environment. What do you think about
that?*

TB: My father is one of those people who has observed, collected,
identified and classified. As an active member of his local fungi
group he has spent many hours in the field collecting specimens for identification and recording. Many hours spent with
the microscope follow, samples are sent to more professionally
trained colleagues and all is meticulously logged. I know others
who choose to focus in similar ways on birds, bats or other flora
and fauna.

On one level I think of this activity as an invaluable way of
recording the environment and in particular providing evidence
of loss or degradation of it. The painstaking work of countless volunteers across the country helps to build a huge body of knowledge and understanding about the natural environment and the
impact of human beings on it.

While I admire the work done by these people and at times
envy the depth of their knowledge, I am not one of them, at this
time of my life. I seem to want to immerse my self in the whole
rather than focus on the specific. For me the experience of the
song of the bird in the moment is more important than being able
to identify the bird that produced the song. So I have a reasonable
amateur knowledge of flora and fauna but no real desire to know
it all, or collect it.

While I'm sure the collectors and categorizers would say that
those activities bring them closer to the natural environment
and it is their way of connecting to it, for me it can be a distraction. However, perhaps my somewhat prejudiced view is beginning to change. I have had a long period of poor health recently,
involving a lot of time lying about in the garden convalescing
and I've become increasingly aware of the insect population in
the garden. On hot days the garden is full of insects, and bumblebees in particular. I am attempting to survey the bumblebee visitors we get and send this information to a bumblebee
conservation group which is monitoring their population– and
threats to it– across the country. I have found it is not easy to get

a bumblebee to sit still in order to find out which of 25 possible bees it could be!

CR: *One aspect of the natural world that people talk about constantly is the weather. This is something that affects all of us, whether in urban or rural locations. What is your experience? Does it affect how you feel, for example?*

TB: I suppose I subscribe to the idea that there is no such thing as bad weather, only bad clothes and equipment! I have spent a lot of time outside in all weathers, heavy downpours, howling gales and freezing blizzards and I have always come away from those experiences with something positive so that I tend to think of the weather as value free. Having said that I don't like overcast grey days when nothing is happening. I can find that depressing.

Once again I'm drawn to extremes. If I could choose, I'd go for the heat for at least three months every summer, like those dry hot days of southern France. I like it when it's too hot to do anything in the middle of the day, with the strong scents of lavender and sage, and when the buzzing of insects forms the background noise in the evening.

But I've had memorable times in the freezing cold too. I once spent the night in the cable car station on the Aiguille du Midi, at 3500 metres, and emerged from the ice tunnel before dawn to start a long walk and scramble on my own along the fine ice and snow ridge above Chamonix, to the Aiguille de Plan. The stars were still out and it was perfectly still, and bitterly cold. The only sound was the crunch of my crampons on the hard snow of the ridge. After an hour I saw the first signs of sunrise as the peaks far off to the east began to turn pink and gold with the coming light. It was magnificent and worth cold fingers and toes for a few hours.

CR: *I wonder if you see any connection between your relationship with the natural environment, in all its complexities, and with the other significant relationships in your life?*

TB: I think of the natural environment as a space in which much of my relating with others can take place. Most of my close friends and my partner share my passion for the natural environment. We walk together, canoe together and head for the hills together. We tend our gardens in wildlife-friendly ways, buy organic food and do the things that other concerned liberals do. In that sense there are shared values and shared concerns that bind us.

In relation to intimacy, the natural environment provides both a place to connect with others, and enhance intimate relationships, and a place to escape to, when relationships get difficult. If I look back at my life many of the high points combine encounters with the natural environment and moments of connection with others. This could be sharing an adventurous day in the mountains with a friend, picking flowers with a child in the countryside or lying under the stars, by a fire, with my partner.

It is also a place to be on my own, to give myself space and time to gather my thoughts, to lick my wounds and then go back and re-engage with the complexities of the human world. The natural environment does not seem complex to me; rather it's a space which is straightforward, predictable in its unpredictability and impersonal in the sense that it is not interested in me.

If I think of the natural environment as a person then in my early years I would have described them as disinterested, challenging, someone for me to knock up against and try to gain attention from. This is interesting because it has obvious parallels for me with my relationship with both of my parents. I saw them, after the age of eight, as distant, hard to reach and withholding. The separation caused by boarding school was handled by them with great awkwardness and lack of warmth. Also they were pre-occupied with my youngest brother, who was born with severe learning difficulties, and who was taking up a huge amount of time and energy at that time.

My response was to withdraw and give up on trying to get what I needed or wanted from them. I didn't struggle or 'make a fuss' with them but maybe I took that need into my relationship with the natural environment. I developed a stoic resignation that I had to look after myself and that it was possible to endure almost any hardship without 'fuss'. That made me a 'good' outdoor enthusiast, able to deal with physically demanding situations, make decisions and take the initiative but perhaps not an easy person to have a relationship with! It left me cut off from knowing and being able to express my own needs either to myself or to others, and at times I was contemptuous of those who could.

As my awareness of these dynamics became clearer so my relationship with the natural environment changed from one of struggle and challenge to one that is more benign and caring, both of myself and the other.

CR: *Right at the start you talked about the ways in which the natural environment is under threat. We are losing habitats and species at an alarming rate. Have you encountered any of this in your own experience?*

TB: Actually it's happening on our doorstep. Below our house are two farms. To the right is a one-thousand acre dairy farm with 500 dairy cows. The pastures on which the cattle graze and that produce feed for the winter are probably between twenty and fifty acres and they have been 'improved' by the heavy use of fertilizers and other chemical inputs. Hedges have been removed over the years to enable bigger machinery to get onto the land. While there is no doubt that this style of intensive farming is efficient and produces high yields you only have to walk through the fields to see that it has also produced a mono-crop prairie-like environment with little biodiversity. Few flowers mean few insects, which mean few birds and bats. Fertiliser and pesticide run-off from farms like that end up in the streams and rivers in the county causing a collapse in fish stocks on the River Wye and Usk. The evidence is clear to see.

To the left of our house is a small sixty-acre farm or small holding. Small fields bounded by traditional hedges are managed in a low input way. The fields are rich in plant species and on warm evenings the air is thick with insects. We can watch house martins feeding in the day and bats at night. The small mammal population is obviously high too, evidenced by the presence of owls hunting in the early mornings.

While I am not naïve about the pressure from the marketplace on farmers to improve efficiency and yields there has to be recognition that continued intensification will have serious consequences for the natural environment.

Globally, the picture is even more worrying, with our insatiable demand for resources of all types putting enormous pressure on the natural world. The oil spillage in the Gulf of Mexico is a perfect example of this. I think all of this gives rise to feelings of anxiety and helplessness amongst ordinary people.

CR: *There is so much cause for concern. What gives you hope?*

TB: Some big farmers are getting the message about environmental damage and their own responsibilities in this area and obviously financial incentives help encourage them to farm their land in a more environmentally friendly way. Locally, nationally and internationally there are many environmental pressure groups doing practical conservation work, raising awareness with the public and putting pressure on governments to protect their natural environments. I think all this helps to ensure that environmental concerns are kept in people's minds.

At the end of the day people will do what they do and the natural environment will look on impassively. It will be here long after the human race has gone and will return to some sort of balance. By cutting ourselves off and ignoring the demands of the natural environment the only thing we risk is, at best, our own well-being, and at worst our own survival.

CR: *I think it would be appropriate to end with some reflection about this 'interview'. How have you experienced it? Has it been a restatement of what you already knew, or taken you into different places?*

TB: I have enjoyed thinking about all this over the last few weeks. It has reminded me how important my relationship with the natural environment has been and in particular how important it was to me as a young person, struggling to make sense of the world and to deal with the challenges life was throwing at me. It has also reminded me of significant moments in my life, peak experiences with others and on my own, which have been stored away.

Our conversation has enabled me to link my experiences in the natural environment with my personal development, and to see those experiences not as something separate, in a box on the side, but as an integral part of who I am and how I became who I am. The conversation has reconfirmed my belief in the power of the natural environment to reconnect us with what is really important in life. It has made me realize there are many different ways that people make this connection; from those who use the natural environment to create challenges for themselves in wilderness areas, to those who seek out the more peaceful and benign aspects, like a picnic in the countryside, to those who connect with it through detailed scientific study, the collectors and categorizers.

I am at a point now in my life when I have been forced to take some time out from my work, for health reasons. It has been an opportunity to reflect on what I've been doing professionally for the last few years and what I want to do in the next period of time. Thinking about my relationship with the natural environment has made me realize that this is something that has been missing from my working life for some time and I intend to explore the possibility of rebuilding that connection in some way.

The experience of writing and reflection has also made me realize that there is a whole area of eco-psychology literature that has passed me by, and that I want to explore this to integrate the counsellor and the 'wild man' in me.

CR: *Tim, thank you.*

Points for reflection

You might like to use this as a template for an internal dialogue, or perhaps conduct a similar interview with a friend, and be interviewed yourself. You may have different questions and areas that you wish to explore, that resonate with your own experiences.

Further resources

On ecopsychology

Roszak, T., Gomes, M., Kanner, A. (eds). (1995). *Ecopsychology: Restoring the Earth, Healing the Mind.* San Francisco: Sierra Club Books.

Rust, M-J. (2008). *Consuming the Earth: Unconscious Processes in Relation to Our Environmental Crisis.* Keynote Lecture for Climate of Change conference, Bristol. http://www.mjrust.net/downloads/Consuming the Earth.pdf

On the natural environment

Deakin, R. (1999). *Waterlog.* London: Chatto and Windus

Deakin, R. (2007). *Wildwood: A Journey Through Trees.* London: Hamish Hamilton Ltd.

Macfarlane, R. (2007). *The Wild Places.* London: Granta Books.

Macfarlane, R. (2003). *Mountains of the Mind.* London: Granta Books.

Getting more involved:

http://www.wildlifetrusts.org/
http://www.wwf.org.uk/
http://www.greenvolunteers.com

10
Developing through Transcendence

Richard Worsley

Beginning with who I am

I am Richard. I am married with two adult children. I love my family. I work as a psychotherapist. I am an Anglican priest. Yet, however important, these are labels and they are on the surface. I sometimes use these labels to flag up approximate versions of my identity, but they are not who I am.

Who I am always goes beyond the labels. The labels will never tell the full story. Yet, who I am is not just a longer story than the labels can tell. It is *inexhaustible*. Who I am is always more than can be told. Thus, when I try to encounter – to meet in the fullness and depth of existence – another human being, I am always bound to fall short. To encounter each other is also to engage with not knowing. There is always more to be said. The more to be said stretches into the past, and as long as I live it stretches into the future too. Yet, the more is always present. The more is not just a little more, but it is uncountable. It is the quality of not being fully known by myself or others.

In this chapter, I put forward the notion that part of our identity as human being centres upon the specific and challenging idea of transcendence. I want to explore this difficult quality of experiencing and existing: I am always more than either of us can say. So are you! For me the attraction of the notion of transcendence is that it is both general and specific. It points clearly to a range of human experiencing and yet it can carry a wide variety of meanings, religious, spiritual and secular.

The attribute of transcendence matters not only for individuals. We live and grow in groups and in society. Therefore, I will suggest that transcendence is closely related to the idea of, and experience of, human encounter. We encounter each other when we move beyond seeing another person as a mere version of ourselves. This involves allowing the other to be very different indeed from us, an aspect of our acceptance of them. In being open to this *otherness* of other people, we find transcendence.

Seeking transcendence

As we train as therapists we are asked through this experience, a number of profound questions. One question is what it is to be human. Unless we can give some answer to this, then we may struggle to accompany another person on their journey towards human wholeness. Another question is what it is to be ethical. Until we see that the other places upon us ethical demands which go beyond ourselves, our interests and our imaginings even, then we cannot offer the unconditional love and care which is at the heart of human wholeness.

The rather difficult idea of transcendence stretches and challenges us to tackle these key questions in new ways. Being ethical is not just a wise professional piece of conduct. It is at the very heart of our meeting with others. In the words of Buber (1958), we can either treat the other as a Thou, with all of the ethical dignity that goes with that, or as an It, a mere tool for our own gratification. This transition from It to Thou, and the rendering conscious of it as well, is near the heart of all counsellor training. We are faced by our clients and by ourselves with the question of transcendence.

I want to add that the question is not necessarily connected with spirituality, which has recently become a popular discourse in counselling (see Moore and Purton, 2006). There are many uses and usages of the word spiritual. Some of them are most valuable while others are trite and muddled. However, the notion of transcendence must not be confused with this. Transcendence is about a going-beyond. We can go beyond many things. I suggest above that the beginning counsellor is called to go beyond two particular ideas. The first is that others are somehow extensions or reflections of ourselves – a sort of narcissism to be overcome. The second is that what it is to be human cannot be reduced to logical-material categories only – mere extensions of biology. To be human is to transcend all neat definitions of our species. It is when we risk transcending our own humanity that we surrender our false certainties and destabilize our discourse about ourselves. Transcendence is an imaging or imagining subversively of what it is to be us.

What might transcendence be?

Let your mind rest on the word: transcendence. What occurs to you? What feelings? Preconceptions? Irritations? Prejudices, even?

Transcendence is a difficult word. Paradoxically, we might need to assert its importance and then be very puzzled as to what it means. This is because the word indicates a set of phenomena which, if we are to understand them, we must first be puzzled by them.

The Latin root of the word means something like a moving through or beyond. I suggest that this root meaning links the word to a profoundly human urge: That is, to cry out 'There must be more than this!' The *cri de coeur* that there must be more is a protest against the reduction of humanity. It can have many meanings and implications. It might mean that life should hold more depth than what is experienced at some points. It might be a plea for human dignity in the face of oppression. It might be a claim that reality is more than meets the eye. It might be a *cri d'amour* towards the divine. Yet, the basic desire to cry out in protest that there must be more is the root fact. Of course, in seeking the *more* that there might be, we could be wholly wrong and misguided, chasing rainbows. Yet, we persist in crying out.

The fact of this cry is at the heart of transcendence. We cry out. What this means, and what truths it relates to are simply different questions from the fact of the cry itself. The cry persists. If it is basic to being human, can we therapists hear this in our clients and ourselves? Can we begin to connect the cry to its potential meanings in all of their variety?

While the notion of transcendence is well attuned to the spiritual and the religious, this is not a necessary connection. Some sorts of transcendences are very matter-of-fact and everyday. Let us consider the case of Tony.

Tony came to me with a serious alcohol problem. In fact, he was about to enter a detoxification and rehabilitation process. He was in his mid-twenties. In the initial session, he said that his well-to-do mother had given him so much of what he wanted. (Father had been off the scene for many years.) He had been encouraged to save, so that, unlike many of his friends, he had a large bank balance after only six or seven years in work. He was deeply ashamed of his drinking. It shamed his family. Yet, as he talked about the money, I realized that he had used drinking to subvert a whole set of his mother's values. I guessed that at heart he was far less materialistic than his mother.

His deep shame at his drinking, and his seeing it as a disease, helped him to find a 'cure'. Detoxification worked. He found a new girlfriend. Life looked up. The content of the counselling seemed riddled with success. Was this Tony, or just the reincarnation of his mother's boy?

After session two, any mention of the money had subsided. It had gone underground. I had a clear hypothesis. For whatever reason, Tony had been deeply dissatisfied with his mother's way of living, her living for money, and his conformity to this. The function of drinking had been in part to undermine this. It worked. When he saw me he was pretty broke.

Before we began to work together, fear and self disgust had led him to want to stop drinking. The old conformity returned, and with it many real and material gains, not to mention his mother's approval. All was well for Tony again.

(Worsley 2009: 157)

At first sight, my work with Tony might not look at all like transcendence. It is not about the mystical, or about God or about the transpersonal. It is, though, very much about what it is for Tony to be Tony, and hence what it is to be human. My suspicion was that Tony wanted to go beyond the confines of his mother's materialism. His life had a felt-sense of values and meaning, but these were constricted by his mother. He had to conform. To the extent that I brought about an uncritical end to his alcohol abuse, we had only managed to collude with mother against Tony. I felt deeply dissatisfied with this, even if it helped his relationships and his liver. I could only hope that he found another way to express freely who he wanted to be. In his dialogue with his mother, I was sort of on the side of the subversive drink. It was not a good way of expressing himself, but it was a clear case of Tony knowing that his mother's ways were simply, as we might say, not *Him*.

Transcendence is neither a thing nor a state, but rather a continuum of qualities of living. In Tony's case, the question of the *more* is about the aims and goals of life. Tony was willing to do himself considerable harm in order to escape the confines of his mother's highly restrictive value system. For him, there had to be more.

The idea of transcendence as I put it forward is deliberately broad. It may include the spiritual, the religious and the secular. It is fair to ask: What does it preclude? It precludes all that reduces being human to the mechanistic, to the objectifying. In the words of Martin Buber (1958), transcendence always points to the Thou of our being and not exclusively to the It that might usurp this.

Transcendence as a concept links the cry that there must be more to a series of life stances or belief systems about the nature of the human act of going beyond. These stances are varied, and they often refer to different levels of life. Thus, going beyond can signal the transcendence of parents' values or of society's meanings. It can point to ecstatic experience or to the love of God. The act of going beyond is unlimited. Why does this matter for therapy? If transcendence is one major quality of being human and if therapy promotes human being and integrity, then therapists have to learn to listen to the transcendent within the life of the client. However, all of us, and not just therapists, are engaged in seeking the depths of others' humanity. This can be by virtue of being engaged with people work, or of simply being human. For Tony, the transcendent values to which he aspired had drowned first in his mother's materialism, then in alcohol, and perhaps lastly, and most regrettably, in my decision to use short-term work to address some narrower view of health than the transcendent. We have to learn to listen to this quality of life – the concealed *more*.

Transcendence and encounter

Therapy, together with so much more human activity, such as learning, caring, growing, co-operating and competing, is rooted in encounter. Encounter matters to social workers, teachers and most other professions, as well as to therapists. We seek to be met fully as people. We want and need this quality of presence and of relating. We live day by day in encountering others. This is why personal development is so important in counsellor training. We can only meet others when we meet ourselves. So let us begin the journey into the possibility of the transcendent by thinking, dreaming, meditating and reflecting upon ourselves.

Points for reflection

Sit quietly and allow yourself to begin to wonder about who you really are. You may find that a fairly dreamy, meandering state is useful.

What aspects of you-being-you can you notice?

Which of these matter the most to you? Feel within you how these are for you.

What metaphors might you use for yourself? Some people can picture themselves as plants or animals, others as less organic or more abstract entities. In particular, does your metaphor cast you as active or passive or neither?

The more we meditate upon our own being, the more we attain to a global idea of who we are: our stories about ourselves; our sense, conscious and otherwise, of our bodies and ourselves; our ability to relate to others; our place within social structures; and much else. While the points for reflection(above) may seem simple on the surface, I hope that you can sense the quality of their inexhaustibility. That is to say, there would never come a time that you would have to stop because you had recognized all that there was to see in yourself.

The fact that we have an indefinite capacity to create ourselves in our lived experience is what makes relating so extraordinary. People as individuals and in society are endless resources, deep gifts both to themselves and others. People cannot be reduced to predictable, describable, comprehensible units. This fact that we experience in encounter at a practical level is also the heart of human transcendence.

For therapists there is a problem. In formulating the rationale of therapy, we have to state some version of what it is to be human. However, this statement is centred upon the distress and hence the dysfunction that brings people to therapy. Therapists' version of what it is to be human tends to be limited. By way of example, we can look at the thinking of Carl Rogers, but what I claim in fact applies to all therapies roughly equally. In looking at the question of the self, Rogers argues that we have a self concept. That is, we have a more or less conscious account of ourselves that we can often report to ourselves. We also have a version of ourselves that is based upon our ability to evaluate incoming information against our instinct for survival and our tendency to actualise and grow. His account is a fairly approximate version of what it is to be a self. However, it is useful in that it chimes with my experience of others in therapy. The rigid self concept may give a very clear, strident verbal account of the self, but this is in tension with lived experience and often the gap, the incongruence between the two, creates stress, which leads to depression. Rogers' account is structured by observing phenomena of mental distress. Despite Rogers' optimistic view of being human, he omits much of transcendence just because it does not immediately appear to relate to therapists' core concerns.

In recent years, this limited description of what it is to be human has been augmented from a number of sources, including philosophy – and in particular, existentialism – religion and spirituality. Yet it is perhaps in Rogers' dialogue with Martin Buber that the challenge of thinking about transcendence comes into its own.

Listening and confirming

On 18 April, 1957, Carl Rogers and Martin Buber, a twentieth century Jewish philosopher, met and conducted a dialogue that was subsequently published (Kirschenbaum and Henderson 1990). Rogers commented that he had much in common with Buber's thinking. However, as the discussion progressed, one area of apparent disagreement emerged, and it is one with fascinating consequences.

Rogers said that he believed that both Buber and he offered acceptance to others. Buber replied that he saw a major difference between them. While Rogers accepted other people as they were, Buber saw himself as going beyond this and accepting others with all of their potentialities. He called this an act of *confirmation*. He saw himself as 'holding' these potentialities at times. While it is not clear to me that Rogers took Buber's point, let us assume for a moment that Buber is right. This means that in the fullness of encounter, sometimes the therapist will know or intuit the potential or different versions of the client from those that the client perceives. In some sense, this is the transcendent. It at least transcends the immediate and highly conditioned self concept of the client, but it may in some versions disclose, for instance, many other truths that the client has not yet appropriated.

Sometimes that which is transcended is the sheer despair felt by the other person. On a number of occasions I will meet someone who exhibits a true self loathing. At those times I might listen within me for the metaphors which embody the loathing. For instance, suicidal ideation, although it has a number of potential meanings, can be seen sometimes as a metaphor for self-hatred, as well as a literal intention. I need to stand out within me against this self rejection and self contempt. There are generalizations that can help, such as the fact that most people who are unsuccessful at suicide come to regret what they intended. But this does not really go deep enough. It is often said that a therapist working with a suicidal client must know why he – the therapist – wants to be alive. Yet beyond this, we must hold within us the potential for vigorous living that we can intuit within the client. This too is transcendence of death. Buber's idea of *confirmation* will be of particular relevance to my case study of Louise, below.

I now want to point to two characteristic forms of communication in which the transcendent can be disclosed: narrative and metaphor.

Transcendence and narrative communication

Transcendence discloses itself in our personal and our cultural narratives. In other words, first we love stories because they take us to places we long to go. Then we learn to find our own stories and, in them, the yearning for the beyond.

I love *Dr Who* and *Star Trek*. I love them because they pierce through time and space, the very things that limit my physical being, but not my imagination. These stalwarts of sci-fi also take us beyond the personal, be it a benevolent time-lord or a Klingon who has come on board with us humans. These are surely the latter day versions of the Greek and Roman gods and heroes.

Yet, there is something sentimental about it. It is too good to be true. So, my favourite sci-fi story turns out to be the *His Dark Materials* trilogy of Philip Pullman. Pullman uses these three novels as a vehicle for his sceptical atheism – exactly not where I am – but in doing so, he symbolizes the mystery of the psychological and beyond. Lyra, the young heroine, and all other children in a universe parallel to ours, have a daemon, a self which lives in the appearance of a mutating animal on their shoulders. We can literally see the self and its shape in heroic response to the world. If only real psychology were this vivid! Pullman writes in epic style, vaguely reminiscent of Milton for his scope of vision, if not of hope. In Pullman, at least we know the acid truth that transcendence and meaning must meet destructive forces in life, if they are to escape the sentimental.

Our longing for the *more* is so often expressed in the stories that we seek out.

Points for reflection

What stories or narratives echo a sense of transcendence for you? It might be sci-fi, popular or otherwise. It might be a novel you have read, or even a poem. Narratives do not have to be in words. Perhaps it is in a painting that something stands out for you, of the *more* for which you yearn. When you have identified a story etc., let yourself meander through it. What does it represent to you? Why does it matter?

Perhaps you can even think of real episodes in your own life that work in a similar fashion.

We move from narrative to metaphor. They have much in common, but metaphors have a particular importance.

Transcendence and metaphor

Why is metaphor so important? The French philosopher, Paul Ricoeur (1975), made an in-depth study of metaphor. He argued that since the time of Aristotle we have made the mistake of seeing metaphor as mere decoration, which it is not. Metaphor carries meaning that can only be conveyed through its typical structure. Metaphor is an image and a likeness. Two unlike things are brought close to each other so that, through our thought, feeling and aesthetic awareness, new truth can reveal itself. At first glance this would suggest that the more thought-provoking a metaphor is, the more evocative it might be.

Some literal statements can be exhausted for meaning very soon. By contrast, Ricoeur says, a metaphor is always open to further contemplation and further elaboration of possible meaning. More can always be said. Ricoeur calls this the *surplus of meaning*. This is of itself not very surprising as an idea, until he adds: It is in the surplus of meaning that the existential significance of the metaphor lays. The deep meaning of metaphor is in its inexhaustible possibilities of further discovery as to how we connect with it.

This coin can be turned over. It is likely that transcendence can only be expressed though metaphor. There is a close link between the existential significance concealed in the surplus of meaning and the cry that there must be more. That metaphor is inexhaustible is a logical quality. However, its corresponding experiential quality is that metaphor is endlessly puzzling. I can never fully grasp or possess its meaning. When I converse with you, you can always open up further aspects of it. Metaphor is a natural vehicle for thinking the transcendent.

How can I hear a metaphor?

If metaphor is essential to an expression of the transcendent, then one version of the question about how therapists can work with the transcendent is to ask how we can hear the metaphors which emerge in the space between us and out clients.

For me, this question begins with a willingness to be puzzled and hence insecure and not all-knowing in my work with clients. Yet, there is more than this. If metaphors render up depth of significance through their surplus of meaning, then I need to know where (or rather how) meaning begins for me. The meaning of life is in part visceral. It stems from what we often call a gut feeling. Eugene Gendlin's (1997) research into the origin of meaning points to a process in which meaning emerges gradually from the gut level, and only after a while crystallizes out as clear, propositional thought. Meaning is firstly felt and only afterwards clarified. More to the point, in some of its aspects meaning can wither if subjected to undue clarification.

I want to illustrate this visceral hearing of a metaphor from the thought of Martin Buber. In 1947 he develops the metaphor of the *narrow ridge* to represent the risk of transcendent listening. The following point for reflection is an illustration of how to listen to a metaphor, as well as a study in the stance that is required to do this.

Points for reflection

The narrow ridge – what can it mean?

The image of the narrow ridge is one used by Martin Buber to express the problems of knowing transcendent human relating – the I-Thou. Below is the text of what he says. It is puzzling, stretching. It is therefore a good metaphor to make us tease out the surplus of meaning. What can you make of it?

> I have occasionally described my standpoint to my friends as the 'narrow ridge'. I wanted by this to express that I did not rest on the broad upland of a system that includes a series of sure statements about the absolute, but on a narrow rocky ridge between the gulfs where there is no sureness of expressible knowledge but the certainty of meeting what remains undisclosed.
>
> (Buber 1947: 184)

Read Buber's comment for its literal meaning. Be aware that it is both about the surplus of meaning and also it is a metaphor that illustrates this.

Now allow your mind to explore the metaphor. Picture a narrow ridge. What do you see? What landscape does this evoke? What are its qualities? What feelings do you attach to it?

What does the word gulf evoke? Physical sensations? Feelings? What is it like to stare into the gulf, the abyss of meaning?

How might the feelings and sensations help you understand the precariousness of knowledge of which Buber speaks?

The secular and the religious

I see the transcendent as both secular and religious. How these are heard and responded to makes for a good encounter in life's existential domain. If the therapist cannot hear the secular, then God-talk will get trapped into a pseudo-religious ghetto. If the therapist cannot hear the religious, then God-talk will simply be excluded from the therapy room (Pargament 2007). I have reached the point of seeing the secular and the religious as two poles of the transcendent. Each pole must be maintained but not at the cost of excluding its polar opposite. This is not just about hearing the client. It is also about the therapist's ability to know these poles of transcendence within themselves.

I want to suggest that each of us, according to our preferred world-view, will operate near the pole where we feel most at ease. This is understandable enough. However, when I was talking about transcendence with a friend of mine who is a long-time companion on my own spiritual journey, he suddenly asked me how I experienced the transcendent in its secular fashion. For a moment, I was astonished! This seemed crucial, and I had not thought of it. While those who are not religious may struggle to regain enough of the religious pole, I can at least promise that those of us who are steeped in religious sensibility have a parallel struggle to give proper life to its polar opposite. Perhaps it is indeed a better metaphor to talk of moving along points on the continuum that link these polar opposites.

I want to illustrate this quality of listening with a case study. But first it is useful to summarize the key points made already about transcendence:

1. There is a basic sense of the transcendent which is found in the cry: There must be more!
2. The transcendent can be heard and responded to in all relating. Such encounter is at the heart of good therapy and other similar disciplines.
3. Many life stances, religious and secular, are compatible with versions of the transcendent. Only a reductionism of the human is not transcendent.
4. The transcendent discloses itself through both narrative and metaphor.
5. The secular and the religious are two poles of a continuum, upon which the transcendent plays. We need to pay attention to both of these poles and their meanings.
6. What we fail to hear as therapists will be kept out of the therapy room.
7. We can only hear others in this respect if we can hear ourselves as well.

Mindful of the transcendent: a case study in listening

The normal focus of a case study would be the client. However, in thinking about Louise, the focus is the therapist, the present writer. Louise is interesting in that she uses the language of God far more readily than many clients of white British heritage. This left me with a double question. What did I understand by Louise's God-talk and its relationship to her other material? Could I steer a course within myself such that I did justice to both polarities of the transcendent? I want therefore to keep the description of work with Louise to a minimum, and then think hard about my own responses to it, as an illustration of listening for the transcendent.

Louise, a professional woman and a perfectionist, came to counselling after a row with her elderly grandparents. This had precipitated another bout of depression. They had accused her – not for the first time – of being uncaring because she could not resolve the issues in her parents' marriage. Within Louise's birth family, her role is to attempt to make peace and to care. Louise's life at home is a story of perpetual ingratitude towards her. She is always on the edge of getting it wrong by her own lights, which has probably led to her perfectionism. Since she cannot win but buys into the task, she is plagued with guilt.

As we explored guilt at some length, I became increasingly puzzled. Where had she felt disapproval? She began to think about school. She said that although neither she nor her parents were religious, she had gone to a Christian school. I think I immediately formed a picture of a school which would represent God and faith as condemnatory, and thus persecutory. Louise assured me that it was not. Her school was a local Church of England primary and it was not at all strict or judgemental. As far as we could ascertain between us, Louise had taken from school an image of God in whom she does not believe. She had then rendered him judgemental much after the image of God in parts of the Old Testament. He was wrathful, but He did not exist. Nevertheless, he stood in judgement against her. She seemed to be in the most curious double-bind.

I often have the image that a person can be seen as having an internal group. The group contains images of the people within the external world, abstract introjects from the outside world and versions of the self. I do not make a distinction between these. The inside world and the outside world are separated by a membrane that is permeable in both directions. All is metaphor and so flexible, an image of the client's phenomenal world.

At first, God seemed like one of Louise's internal personae whom I did not understand. He was a metaphor, but for what? I persisted with the image of

God as a metaphor needing to be dealt with. So did Louise. (What did we mean by 'dealt with?' Negotiated? Dispatched?) She has persisted with the idea of God as "negotiable" in a way that has taken her and me, time and again, into the area of God as good or as bad. After a while, I reflected to her that this seemed as if God were ceasing to be a mere metaphor, and that she was getting to be really interested in finding out what sort of God might be worth believing in. She agreed.

From session to session we moved to and fro between some God-talk and rather a lot more about Louise and her family and her stuckness. We spent quite a bit of time thinking about how Louise related to her family. I could hear how she had to "buy" their approval by being useful, their rescuer.

I concluded one session by saying to her: You confuse being needed with being loved. This remained with her. At the beginning of the next session she said: That's it, I think. She was able to unpick, for the first time, how influential her mother's wider family was in their punitive ensnaring of her and others. She was able to think more freely about letting go of the vice-like grip of some family ties. For the first time, there is a sense for me of dawning resolution.

I want to begin thinking about my response to Louise in terms of the following words from my brief account, above: *I reflected to her that this seemed as if God were ceasing to be a mere metaphor, and she was getting to be really interested in finding out what sort of God might be worth believing in. She agreed.* It is my phantasy that the reader will all too swiftly conclude: He would say that, wouldn't he? We each carry with us our own worldview, more or less critically. In our post-modern and post-liberal society, where there is no longer a consensus – however superficial – or predominant worldview, there might be some idea that we are more open to others. I think to the contrary. We rush to defend or promote our own worldview. So, as a Christian, I would say that, wouldn't I?

Well, actually, no! It took an awful lot of guts on my part, not to mention careful listening, to make this reflection or observation. It would have been easy for me to exclude from the room that which I might be afraid of promoting, in the same way that an atheist might have a similar fear of observing that which she literally does not believe in. Therefore at the heart of talking with Louise is the problem of being true to both poles of the transcendent.

I must not act to proselytize, nor must I block the client's route to faith in God, whoever I am. This is about being agnostic – in a proper sense – for long enough.

But before moving into this, let us note the two stances which can be found within the world of therapy that have to be eschewed in order to listen for the transcendent. Some forms of so-called Christian counselling (such as Adams 1986) work often by cognitive-behavioural methods to ensure that the client adopts the religious position of the counsellor. This is specifically what I did not want to do. I hope I do not even need to explain why! The classical Freudian is also prone to manoeuvre the client, this time into the rejection of religious world-views, by the psychological reduction of God to a symptom of the client's pathology. In this interpretative process, the therapist leaves no room for shared agnosticism.

Agnosticism, by contrast, aims to keep open the field between client and therapist. It is not about pretending to have not made up our minds about God or anything else for that matter. It is about finding an internal space in which deliberate ambivalence can be created. I need to be radically unsure about what the narratives and metaphors might mean, and thus to be open to any prompting whatsoever from Louise. I want to suggest that client and therapist, at moments of real, existential depth, resonate with each other. (This is of course a metaphor!) I postulate that if I can keep a clear space within me to hear whatever emerges, then Louise will do the same.

When therefore I took the risk of reflecting to Louise my hearing her moving away from God as mere metaphor, I was opening a space within us both for the possibility that, while God never ceases to be a metaphor, He is also more of a metaphysical reality. The risk, the art form here, is in offering the possibility as to where Louise might be going, but without insisting on it being the preferred – or the best avoided – meaning.

To open up this space in the matrix of meaning between Louise and me, I have to first set aside any preferred outcome. This includes setting aside any preferred meaning for the word God. This is as crucial for the atheist as for the theist. I then picture Louise as seeking meaning, of which there is infinitude! But, because meaning comes into being *between* people rather than within an individual, then I need to stand with all of my own meanings, before Louise, as much face-to-face and side-by-side. This is encounter as Buber speaks of it. Louise and I are then resources for each other. It is in keeping the space clear enough that we do not propagandize each other. It is in keeping the space rich enough in meanings from us both that we can nurture each other.

The outcome of the therapy was that Louise came to recognize that careful thinking about her mother's family gave her space to choose to seek love rather than approval. Love itself is a transcendent quality, for to be loved is both practical and finite, and absolute and non-finite. I am left at the end of my work with Louise knowing that the shift in

God-image seems to be intimately linked with her ability to conceptualize her family in a more productive way, to be more sceptical of her own need to seek approval, and to begin to think of herself as loveable rather than worthy.

I am not only open, but at the end of the work, frankly puzzled, as to which version of *there must be more* matters and will matter to Louise. It is one of the frustrating things of listening for the transcendent that the openness within the field will not tell me – or even Louise – for certain which version works for her. She may not yet know. After all, this is the transcendent! It might be that what Buber called confirmation is about keeping open with the client a whole range of potential meanings.

Conclusion – the negative way

I have pondered long whether there are positive steps to listening within and beyond ourselves for the transcendent. I have reluctantly come to see that I cannot easily name them. Rather, the negative way is to be preferred. How do we block ourselves from hearing the transcendent? There are characteristic mistakes which blind us to this aspect of being human.

We must learn to renounce certainty, and come to inhabit the narrow ridge of which Martin Buber speaks. This means that we must first let go of any desire to reduce being human to measurable categories. We must embrace being surprised by the other person, radically astonished at what will reveal itself. We must be prepared to find and not block our own cry that there must be more. Even if we can be free from the longing to be certain, and to inhabit the narrow ridge, we must be able to desire to be two-eyed, and to see the transcendent as both religious and secular at the same time. This means relinquishing any reductionist interpretation of the data of our own and others' beliefs. We who are atheists must see the divine in others. We who are faithful to God must release our grasp on her. We need to do justice to both poles, to the whole continuum.

We must also let go of our craving for the literal. This too can be false security. We need the belief-structures to which we cling, and we also have to move to the beyond. I must let go of a reluctance to listen to metaphor and narrative, but I must also let go of any reluctance to allow another person's truth to have a literal status. I must hear both narrative and metaphor as open, so that others' truths have the same status as my own.

When I can hold in my mind a string of possibilities for the client, including the client's own potential, her future, and be deeply puzzled by what might be the case, I as listener open up a space within me, and a space between her and me, in which there will emerge what will emerge.

Acknowledgement

I am grateful to Louise for giving me permission to use a small part of her work with me. Her name and details have been changed to protect her identity, but the process is as far as I can judge faithful to the shared reality between her and me.

Further resources

The following two books put the confusing discourse of spirituality into some useful context:

Moore, J. and Purton C. (eds.). (2006). *Spirituality and Counselling: Experiential and Theoretical Perspectives*. Ross-on-Wye: PCCS Books.
Schreurs, A. (2001). *Psychotherapy and Spirituality: Integrating the Spiritual Dimension into Therapeutic Practice*. London: Jessica Kingsley Publishing.

However the real resources for thinking about transcendence are many, and often fictional. They are therefore personal. I find the following resources useful.

Buber, M. (1958). *I and Thou*. Edinburgh: T & T Clarke.
Dostoevsky, F. (2004). *The Idiot*. Harmondsworth: Penguin Classics.
Eliot, TS. (2001). *Four Quartets*. London: Faber.
Levinas, E. (1999). *Totality and Infinity: An Essay on Exteriority*. Pittsburgh: Duquesne University Press.
O'Donohue, J. (1999). *Anam Cara: Spiritual Wisdom from the Celtic World*. (2nd ed.) London: Bantam.
Thomas, R.S. (1997). *Mass for Hard Times*. Tarset; Bloodaxe. In particular "Migrants" (p. 80).

Media other then the written word are important, just because the word, the logical, is transcended. For me, music in particular touches the felt-self without intervening specific meanings. Chapter 6, Developing through Music, is relevant here.

11
Developing through This Book

Chris Rose

Being interested in who we are and who others might be is not a short-term project. It involves a set of attitudes and behaviours that value curiosity and enquiry, as well as the ability to let go of certainties and re-examine our truths. It disturbs and challenges us to stay open to the many contexts that we experience and to acknowledge the impossibility of 'self' without 'other'. Developing our awareness of the complex inter-relationships, identifying our own contributions and struggling to engage in ways congruent with our values – all this, you might say, is about being alive.

If this is beginning to sound overly romantic, it is easily balanced by the recognition that we are multiple selves. When I write about being open, curious, engaged, vital, of course I am referring to one aspect of self. Nobody is so one dimensional that they are consistently like this, rather than at times defensive, cross or indifferent. The book has attempted to catch the attention of the curious character while making space for those other, less co-operative ones who may sabotage and obstruct the development of self awareness.

Alongside this theme of the multiple self, often expressed by the metaphor of the internal group, sits the other central message of the book. We are created in and by social, biological, political, economic and natural environments. In turn, we are part of their creation. We are who we are in the contexts of others; there is no self without other.

This concluding chapter returns to the starting point to re-iterate the ways in which we are shaped by our societies and cultures. It then considers how we might push beyond the confines of existing self awareness into new territories.

Introductions and beyond

Greg is attending the first session of his counselling course, and he is sitting in a circle of people that he has never met before, but who will be his fellow students for the next two years. The tutor suggests that they introduce themselves, but they have all said a great deal without opening their mouths. Like the others, Greg's physical appearance, age, gender and race have all been communicated already. There may be errors to be subsequently corrected, but Greg has been positioned in relation to key markers in society. He is male, white, looks to be in his early 30s and he is apparently physically fit. His ginger hair and pale freckled skin mark him out as belonging to a Northern European racial group and in certain circles make him a target for mockery. When he speaks, the Birmingham accent locates him geographically. Additional clues come from the t-shirt with the Amnesty International logo and the shining wedding ring that he frequently turns around his finger.

The introductions begin with the woman with cropped hair and red earrings telling them her name and occupation, that she has two teenage children and that her hobbies include restoring furniture and gardening. This seems to set the format, and the next few people give similar sorts of information about themselves.

Greg was christened Edward after his paternal grandfather, a man whom he never met. It was a name that he came to dislike and when he moved to secondary school he announced that he wished to be known as Greg, his second name. Our names are the key words in introducing ourselves, and our relationship to these words is interesting. They are usually our parents' choice, perhaps dictated by family connections or contemporary fashion, and we inhabit them with varying degrees of ownership.

Occupation follows gender and race as one of the most important indicators used to answer the 'Who are you?' question. It can be used as a shorthand way of conveying several types of information such as social status and class, educational attainment, economic well-being, as well as ethical attitudes. Occupation, earnings and possessions come together in recognized and predictable patterns that are used to differentiate one group from another. The fact that there are many exceptions to the formulas does not render them obsolete.

Whether or not we have children – our family status – forms another marker in locating self and other, and this may or may not be accompanied by information about partnerships. Locating the self in the context of personal relationships can be a sensitive area but it is vital information in understanding self and others. Greg's wedding ring has already signalled his relationship status and it is part of his public presentation of self. The networks of intimate relationships, particularly family, are central to our own self image and that of others.

We locate ourselves and others in the social sphere, acknowledging relationships with particular sections of society and demonstrating positions in various hierarchies. All of this is crucial, but it does not necessarily articulate our uniqueness. This comes from the particular way in which the many groups that we belong to, family, gender, race, work, age, social class, religion, interests, activities and so forth, intersect and interact. The 'self' here is like a social fingerprint, a unique pattern derived from many aspects held in relationship with each other.

Our uniqueness comes as well through the ways in which we take up our myriad group memberships. Although we are all born or grow into certain positions within the structure of society, we can at times assert an individual presence through the ways in which we occupy this position. This is very much affected by resources: Greg, for example, as a middle class, educated, white, able-bodied male is in a relatively strong position to negotiate his own style. He cannot escape from his identity as a 'white man', for example, but he has some choices concerning the type or style of 'white man'. Introducing information about hobbies and interests, as well as wearing t-shirts with logos, are ways of conveying something of that style, those unique aspects of ourselves that distinguish us from the broader picture.

It comes to Greg's turn to introduce himself and he has a dilemma. He could play by the rules and give the now formulaic response – name, occupation, family, hobbies; he could puncture the serious atmosphere by saying something witty, which is one of his characteristic ways of engaging with people; he could take the risk of saying something very personal and potentially exposing; he could follow the lead of the man sitting next to him who gave his name and said he did not wish to say any more at the moment. All of these responses would reveal some aspect of him to the group and none would be fraudulent in any way.

His choice will reflect the context. By now Greg will have gathered information not just through what has been said, but in all the other cues, signals and resonances that operate whenever people are together. He will have identified certain people who he thinks are interesting or off putting, and knows who he will look out for in the coffee break. Even though he may not be aware of it, his introductory statement will emerge as a response to the interpersonal environment that he is in.

This begins the process of relating that develops through mapping, mirroring, resonating patterns of mutual interaction, into the complex and shifting landscapes of intimate relationships. We learn much about ourselves as we begin to pay attention to the ways in which we find ourselves in repeated scenarios, playing out familiar roles in partnership with others engaged in similar processes. Past experience, present circumstances and predicted futures work together to shape our interactions. Much of the work of self awareness leads us back into our memories of significant early relationships to discover that there is more to the stories we tell about ourselves and our families than we ever thought. It casts new light upon subsequent relationships and behaviours, and then illuminates how we act today.

Taking it further

If this phrase conjures up a linear image, then I would want to replace it with a spiral. Perhaps in all learning, but particularly in this area, we are continually revisiting familiar material. Anyone who has kept a diary or journal over any length of time will recognize the experience of looking back through the pages to discover that today's great revelation was also discovered many months or years ago! Moments of clarity and understanding seem to lose their brightness and sink into obscurity, to be rediscovered anew. It can seem as if we are ploughing the same field all the time, going over and over the same ground and not recognizing it. The image of the spiral is more hopeful, because it conveys the notion that we can find ourselves at very similar points in the curve but they are at different stages of the spiral. Time and context move us inexorably along the spiral so that what we may be experiencing seems repetitive, but there are always differences, however subtle.

This is seen clearly in long-term psychotherapy, in which experiences are revisited and re-explored to reveal aspects that had not been recognized in earlier accounts. Paying close attention to that which seems tediously familiar can often be rewarded with new insights and connections, particularly if the context and the process are taken into account. So, for example, revisiting the experience of introducing yourself to a group of strangers could reveal more about the messages you might have conveyed and the choices you made in describing yourself.

Despite this, in all learning there comes a point at which we reach a plateau; intellectually we know that there is more, but we cannot find the means to access it. What we are looking for might be described as 'getting beyond' or 'getting under the surface'. Usually this refers to the task of accessing something out of awareness, but it may also have echoes of transcendence (Chapter 10). The images are often archaeological, as in 'depth' or 'layers', a legacy of the Freudian influence both upon popular culture and psychodynamic thinking. This creates an image of the unconscious as lying hidden beneath our conscious awareness, unavailable to scrutiny except through particular techniques.

Neuroscientists describe the relationship between conscious and unconscious processes not in terms of layers but as continuously interacting systems. Edelman and Tononi (2000) use the metaphor of a president and cabinet, in which each minister receives messages from his department that influence policy but they are never themselves on the agenda. There is an interesting parallel with the internal group, thinking of each character as being influenced by unconscious communications that are never directly addressed but that are highly relevant to the communication between group members. How might we find out more?

Creative spaces

In response to this question I want to look at three different areas of playing, dreaming and meditating, with particular reference to playing with words, dream work in groups and mindfulness. These all, in different ways, involve a type of creative experience that can overturn the conventions of everyday life. They liberate us from the domination of the sensible, logical, rational and sequential, into a space where distinctions between what is 'real' and what is 'not real' do not need to be made.

Playing

Winnicott calls this area 'transitional space', the borderlands between what is 'internal' and what is 'external'. He saw psychotherapy as providing a transitional space in which analyst and patient, therapist and client were able to play. Playing enables creativity, which for Winnicott was the route to self discovery. In his eyes, it was essential that the therapist had the capacity to play (Winnicott 1971).

Playing, whether with sounds, images or words, has featured in many parts of this book. It is one of the most important areas in self development and requires nurturing in the face of pressures of time management, regulation and economic efficiency. It is a capacity developed in relationship: We can only play alone because we have learnt to play with, and in the presence of, another. Those who are unable to play are likely to have lacked this developmental experience as children and may need to learn the capacity in the process of therapy itself (Youell 2008).

Points for reflection

What are the ways in which you play? What are your favourite toys?

How might you 'play' as a counsellor or psychotherapist? Can you. describe your state of mind when playing?

Playing with words

Playing involves taking risks, letting go and allowing something new to emerge. These are also present in the state of mind that Bion (1965) refers to as 'reverie' and Foulkes (1984) refers to as 'free floating attention', in which ideas and images are allowed to swim into view without censorship. Like Winnicott, they are exploring the ways in which we may communicate from the unconscious aspects of ourselves directly to the unconscious aspects of another. Freud's (1900) idea of free association, in which the patient uncovers their own underlying unconscious structure through a trail of images and words, has been set into an interactive context in which the therapist too is following their own trail and using it in the communication. Reik's (1948) 'listening with the third ear' is another well-known description of this unconscious-to-unconscious communication in the psychoanalytic setting. It involves an active receptiveness to images and metaphors that arise in conversation, that are related to but not the same as the original comment. These communications are fed by the complex inter-relationships of our physical selves and the ways in which we resonate at different levels with embodied others.

Conversations with ourselves are central to the development of self awareness, and these ways of communicating can enrich our explorations. Paying attention to the words we choose in talking with ourselves can take us along some interesting pathways. For example, when an internal voice is heard to say 'you are making a pig's ear out that', or 'that was a piece of cake'; or the voice uses powerful words such as 'batter' or 'jerk', we can work with these. We need to give ourselves permission to make links and associations, however illogical or silly

they might seem, because they have the potential to expand our understandings.

Metaphors offer a particularly rich source of understanding, linking
and holding together truths and fictions, internal and external realities.
(See Chapter 10 for further discussion.) If we can tolerate ambiguity
and paradox without rushing to understand, new insights emerge. We
do not have to know, rather to give time to gather, explore and play
with enough material to enable shape and coherence to develop (Cox
and Theilgaard 1997). The 'internal group' is itself a metaphor that can
generate a multiplicity of associations and responses, working together
to create a rich and multifaceted definition.

Dreams

Dreams can be thought of as a particular type of metaphor that connects
experiences, thoughts and emotions in unconventional ways. There are
varied hypotheses concerning the nature of dreams. For example, they
represent dilemmas that we are trying to solve; they are messages from
parts of ourselves or from some spiritual source; they are attempts to
process experiences and emotions; they are the rumblings in the pipes
while the boiler is on standby.

Whatever we consider to be its nature or origin, it is never possible to
accurately represent the dreaming experience. Our attempts to describe
them, in words or images, are creative acts and can be reflected upon in
the same ways as other imaginative creations. Although we may learn
much by ourselves in the process of this reflection, other people can
help in taking things further. This is the case in many areas, but dreaming is used here as a particular example.

Others can provide an emotionally supportive context where their
interest encourages a closer and more detailed articulation of the dream.
New aspects are remembered or created that enlarge the content and
help to recapture the emotional tone. This expands the range of possible associations that can be facilitated in conversation with another
person. Depending on the relational context, the other person may
contribute their own associations. These may be made in the light of
their knowledge about the dreamer: 'That made me think of the story
you told me about your brother'; they may also contribute their own
personal reactions: 'If that was my dream I would feel very frightened'.
Using the images and emotional tone that the dream evokes in others
can take the dreamer further in understanding the meanings and significance of the dream.

Dream work in groups

This can be developed in a small group setting, and there are various models available for this type of dream work (Hill 2004; Ullman 1996; Cushway and Sewell 1992). The following is a basic format that can be used by friends or trusted colleagues to learn more about themselves using their dreams.

The group sit in a circle and one person recounts a dream, without any inter-pretations or associations. The group may ask briefly for clarification, but they may not contribute any associations or ideas at this stage. The dreamer then sits out of the circle and the group discusses their own responses to the dream. After a specified time, the dreamer rejoins the group and talks about their reaction to the group discussion. This format is then repeated in turn by the other group members, and as the meeting progresses, common themes usually emerge that add further layers of understanding for all the participants.

Points for reflection

This is something you might like to try for yourself. A small group of three or four people works best, and you will need to allow at least two hours for the conversation. The group will need to decide on time periods, 5–10 minutes only for questions, for example, and 20 minutes for the group discussion. You may want to elect one person to facilitate and keep the time boundaries. This role can rotate if you meet on several occasions.

The search for understanding in a reliable group context generates powerful resonances and insights, and it has many applications. The focus may be dreams, including daydreams and lucid dreams, or other creative products such as writings, art works (see Chapter 7), movement and musical compositions. In all these areas the presence of others widens and deepens the possible range of emotional and intellectual responses, often taking us off in new and unexpected directions.

Group learning demonstrates again the fundamentally social nature of personal development and can be a highly effective means of taking things further. It is a context within which possibilities enlarge, where instead of 'an answer' there appear many threads and interconnections raising more questions. In itself it is a creative space.

Mindfulness and meditation

A different sort of creative space involves letting go and sitting back rather than active pursuit. Mindfulness techniques are increasingly employed in therapeutic settings to enable clients to manage disturbing emotions and thoughts and they can also be used as a part of personal development. Christopher and Maris (2010) talk about using these techniques in counselling training and their benefits in terms of developing self awareness, relating with others and self care.

Learning to pay attention to the experience of the moment, to bodily sensations, thoughts and emotions without judging or reacting is in itself calming and has a physiological impact. There are links here with Gendlin's (1981, 1997) idea of 'focusing', strengthening the awareness of bodily states and their relationship to emotion. One positive outcome is an increased sense of being grounded and connected to the body.

Mindfulness techniques strengthen the capacity to tolerate physical and emotional discomfort; by adopting an observing position, the discomfort can usually be felt to peak and then subside. This increased ability to remain focused and calm in the presence of distress has obvious benefits, both in attending to the self and attending to others. It makes it less important to defend against persecutory voices and opens up space to hear other less dominating voices. In this way mindfulness offers another way of appreciating the range of internal conversation and noise that characterizes our normal waking experience. Being able to hear the internal chatter without being caught up with any particular voice is a skill that not only benefits us but increases our ability to pay attention to the client's multiple voices also.

Mindfulness techniques also contribute to nurturing the self and they are particularly useful in situations in which therapists are exposed to high levels of disturbing emotion over lengthy periods of time. Undoing the link between the flow of experience and its content, accepting whatever is in the flow and moving on to the next moment, can create a sense of calm and peace; at the same time, the act of paying attention to the present moment can enliven and invigorate. Being able to appreciate each moment as something that has never happened before can be particularly refreshing in a work situation in which all seems too familiar and difficult.

Mindfulness techniques derive from meditation and they have many common features, but different aims. In meditation, the practice continues until a state of silence and emptiness can be achieved. Few attain this level of awareness as it requires prolonged practice, but it is a state of being that has been written about not just in the Buddhist tradition but all religious faiths. The 'self' that we experience in our everyday lives becomes not who we are at these points. Instead there may be a heightened sense of unity with all things, an experience of 'one-ness', an encounter with the Other. The experience of the non-self seems a fitting place to draw to a conclusion this journey into self awareness.

Conclusion

Books and their readers are bound together in a particular type of relationship, mediated by the written word. It can readily become a one-way conversation in which the reader's voice is drowned out by the text. Here we have tried to actively engage your curiosity about the self and in doing so it is hoped a relationship has developed. Whether it has been a long-term one, reading the book from cover to cover, or a more fleeting encounter with a chapter here and there, it remains a relationship that can be learnt from.

The book, like the internal group, has different voices that will provoke a variety of responses in the multiple selves of the readers. Thinking about your own reactions to both the content and the style of the book can prove fruitful territory. For example, your reaction to the suggested activities may open up an interesting internal debate about compliance and rebellion. Their purpose was to encourage your own examination and enquiry, and it is hoped that at this stage you can apply this to your reaction to the book. Those aspects that you enjoyed, or disliked – what can they tell you about yourself? Which chapters engaged you and which did not? Which voices did you find easy or hard to listen to? Perhaps there were parts of the book that you felt did not apply to you. Why might that have been so? Your likes and dislikes, agreements and disagreements, connections and failures to connect are all valuable responses to be explored further.

Finally, a book that places such emphasis upon context needs to consider its own. In our own lives, it is always difficult to appreciate the bigger picture that we are immersed within and that shapes our sense of self. Often we need the benefits of hindsight to see more clearly. Trying to gain some overview of society is similarly problematic, and history will make its own judgements. However there appears to be a dominant theme in the present context of psychotherapy and counselling that elevates a medicalized view of mental health and marginalizes others. At the same time as 'talking therapies' are increasingly accepted and demanded, they run the risk of becoming limited in choice and formulaic.

Cultural and economic pressures bear down upon the space for reflection and discussion that is vital to prevent the 'talking therapy' losing sight of both the person of the client and the person of the therapist. Much of this book has been concerned with valuing reflective space, but for many practicing counsellors and psychotherapists there is an ongoing struggle to ensure that they are given enough time – first to engage with clients at depth, and second to process the impact that client contact has upon them.

This is more than the required minimum supervision time, however valuable that may be. Colleagues need space to reflect together upon their work, its impact and its setting; to find creative solutions for the particular challenges that their context presents them with; to pay attention to their own personal and professional needs; to stay interested and engaged and to reflect upon the bigger picture.

Through this wider vision we see a growing attitude that we have rights and entitlements that extend into the area of health, and that all things must be treatable. This makes it more difficult to acknowledge that our capacity to mend, fix, heal and restore is severely limited. Experienced, thoughtful counsellors and psychotherapists of all persuasions know the psychological, philosophical, ethical and practical complexities of 'helping people to feel better'. Poverty, ill health, poor housing, lack of education, prejudice, injustice and degraded environments are not brushed aside by medication, or by learning how to think differently. Neither are the things that help restore and maintain a person's sense of well-being the sole product of therapy – being part of a network of relationships, having some sense of purpose, engaging in meaningful activity, finding a place within the human community – all these experiences are fundamental.

Psychotherapy at its best can facilitate these life-enhancing connections by creating one connection in the room through listening, understanding, empathizing and challenging. Our own ability to make connections transcends any knowledge of models, medicine or technique and this ability resides in 'who we are'. The more we grasp of our own complexity, the better able we are to hear and relate to that of others.

Self awareness is not so much an achievement but more a commitment to a process. It can be challenging, upsetting, serious, frustrating and hard work; but it can also be nurturing, creative, fun, liberating and exciting. What we know is infinitesimal in comparison to what we do not, and it constantly changes through time and circumstance. There will always be more to explore.

Further resources

On dreams and dreaming

Cushway, D. and Sewell, R. (1992). *Counselling with Dreams and Nightmares.* London: Sage.

Hill, C. (2004). *Dream work in Therapy: Facilitating Exploration, Insight and Action.* Washington DC: American Psychological Assoc. Press.

On metaphor

Cox, M. and Theilgaard, A. (1997). *Mutative Metaphors in Psychotherapy: The Aeolian Mode.* London: Jessica Kingsley Publishers.

Knowles M. and Moon, R. (2006). *Introducing metaphor.* Oxon UK: Routledge.

Any poetry that appeals to you.

On mindfulness

For a comprehensive review of mindfulness in the field of therapy see Mace, C. (2007). Mindfulness in Psychotherapy: An Introduction. *Advances in Psychiatric Treatment. vol. 13, 147–154.*

Accessible online at http://apt.rcpsych.org/cgi/reprint/13/2/147.pdf

Gunaratana, H. (2002). *Mindfulness in Plain English.* Boston: Wisdom Publications.

Germer, C., Siegel, R. and Fulton, P. Eds. (2005). *Mindfulness and Psychotherapy.* New York: The Guilford Press.

Bibliography

Ablack, C. J. (2008). The body-mind dynamics of working with diversity. In: *Contemporary Body Psychotherapy: The Chiron Approach*, Ed. Hartley, London: Routledge.

Adams, J.E. (1986). *Competent to Counsel: Introduction to Nouthetic Counseling.* Grand Rapids, MI.: Zondervan.

Adolphs, R. (2006). 'What is special about social cognition?' In Cappioppo, J.V. *Social Neuroscience: People thinking about thinking people.* Cambridge, Mass: MIT Press.

Asch, S. E. (1956). 'Studies of independence and conformity: A minority of one against a unanimous majority'. *Psychological Monographs*, 70.

Austin, J. L. (1962). *How To Do Things With Words: The William James lectures delivered at Harvard University in 1955*, ed. J. O. Urmson. Oxford: Clarendon.

BACP. (2010). *Ethical Framework for Good Practice in Counselling and Psychotherapy.* Lutterworth: BACP.

Balmforth, J. (2009). 'The weight of class: the clients' experiences of how perceived differences in social class between counsellor and client affect the therapeutic relationship', *British Journal of Guidance and Counselling*, 37: 3, 375–386.

Barnes, J. (2009). *Nothing to be Frightened Of.* London: Vintage.

Beauvoir, S. (1989). *The Second Sex. Translated by H. M. Parshley.* New York: Vintage.

Behr, H., and Hearst, L. (2005). *Group Analytic Psychotherapy: A Meeting of Minds.* London: Whurr Publishers.

Benjamin, J. (1990). *Recognition and destruction: an outline of intersubjectivity. Psychoanalytic Psychology*, Vol. 7(Suppl), 33–46.

Berne, E.M. (1994). Games People Play. New York: Grove Press

Bettelheim, B. (1982*). Freud and Man's Soul.* London: Penguin.

Bion, W. (1965). *Transformations: Change from Learning to Growth.* London: Heinemann.

Bolton G.(1999). Therapeutic Potential of Creative Writing:Writing Myself. London: Jessica Kingsley (2010). Reflective Practice: Writing and Professional development. London:Sage

Bowlby, J. (1969). *Attachment and Loss 1: Attachment.* New York: Basic Books.

Bowlby, J. (1973) *Attachment and Loss 2: Separation: Anxiety and Anger.* New York: Basic Books.

Bowlby, J. (1980) *Attachment and Loss 3: Sadness and Depression.* New York: Basic Books.

Bowlby, J. (1997) *Attachment: Volume One of the Attachment and Loss Trilogy.* London: Random House, Pimlico.

Brazier, D. (1993). The Necessary Condition is Love: Going beyond the self in person-centred therapy. In D. Brazier (ed.) *Beyond Carl Rogers*. London: Constable, 72–91.

Bromberg, P. (1996). 'Standing in the Spaces: The Multiplicity of Self and the Psychoanalytic Relationship'. *Contemporary Psychoanalysis* 3: 2 608–636.

Brown, D. (2006). *Resonance and Reciprocity*. Hove: Routledge.

Buber, M. (1947). *Between Man and Man* (trans. Ronald Gregor Smith). London: Kegan Paul.

Buber, M. (1952). *I and Thou*. Edinburgh: T. & T. Clark.

Burkitt, I. (2008). *Social Selves: Theories of Self and Society*. 2nd edition. London: Sage.

Burns, L. (2009). *Literature and Therapy*. London: Karnac.

Butler, J. (1993). *Bodies that Matter*. New York and London: Routledge.

Bytheway, B. (2010). 'Ageing and Ageism', in Giddens A. (ed). *Sociology: Introductory Reader*. MA: Polity Press.

Cappioppo, J.V. (2006). *Social Neuroscience: People thinking about thinking people*. Cambridge Mass: MIT Press.

Christopher, J. and Maris, J. (2010). Integrating mindfulness as self-care into counselling and psychotherapy training. *Counselling and Psychotherapy Research*, 10:2 114–125.

Conard N.J, Malina M., and Munzel S. (2009). *Nature* 460, 695–696 (6 August 2009) doi:10.1038/460695a; Published online 5 August 2009.

Cox, M and Theilgaard, A. (1997). *Mutative Metaphors in Psychotherapy: The Aeolian Mode*. London: Jessica Kingsley Publishers.

Crossley, N. (1996). *Intersubjectivity: The Fabric of Social Becoming*. London: Sage.

Cushway, D. and Sewell, R. (1992). *Counselling with Dreams and Nightmares*. London: Sage.

Dalal, F. (1998). *Taking the Group Seriously*. London: Jessica Kingsley.

Dale, S. (2009). The Grilling of Mr B. *Therapy Today*, 20(7).

Damasio, A. R. (1994). *Descartes' Error*. New York: Grosset/Putnam.

Deakin, R. (1999). *Waterlog*. London: Chatto and Windus.

Deakin, R. (2007). *Wildwood: A Journey Through Trees*. London: Hamish Hamilton Ltd .

Dunn, J. (1988). *The Beginnings of Social Understanding*. Oxford: Blackwell.

Edelman, G. and Tononi, G. (2000). *A Universe of Consciousness: How Matter Becomes Imagination*. New York: Basic Books.

Eigen, M. (2005). *Emotional Storm*. Middletown: Wesleyan University Press.

Elias, N. (1991). *The Society of Individuals*. Tr. Edmund Jephcott. Oxford: Basil Blackwell.

Elliot, A. (2007). *Concepts of the Self*. 2nd edition. Cambridge: Polity Press.

Etherington, K. (2007). *Trauma, Drug Misuse and Transforming Identities: A Life Story Approach*. London: Jessica Kingsley.

Fairbairn, W.R. (1952). *Psychoanalytic Studies of the Personality*. London: Tavistock.

Fairbairn, W.R. (1954). *An Object Relations Theory of the Personality*. Oxford UK; Basic Books.

Folkes-Skinner, J., Elliot R., Wheeler, S. (2010). 'A Baptism of Fire': A qualitative investigation of a trainee counsellor's experience at the start of training.' *Counselling and Psychotherapy Research 10 (2):* 83–92

Foulkes, S.H. (1984). *Therapeutic Group Analysis*. London: Karnac.

Freud, S. (1900). *The Interpretation of Dreams*. Standard edition. London: Hogarth Press.

Freud, S. (1930). 'Civilization and its discontents' in Freud, S. (1991) *Civilization, Society and Religion*, Vol. 12, Penguin Freud Library, London: Penguin.

Frith C. and Wolpert D. (2003). *The Neuroscience of Social Interaction: Decoding, Influencing and Imitating the Action of Others*. Oxford: Oxford University Press.

Gallese, V. (2004). 'The manifold nature of interpersonal relations: the quest for a common mechanism', in *The Neuroscience of Social Interaction*, Frith & Wolpert, eds. Oxford: Oxford University Press.

Gallese, V. (2009) 'We-ness, Embodied Simulation, and Psychoanalysis: Reply to Commentaries,' *Psychoanalytic Dialogues*, 19: 580–584.

Gendlin, E.T. (1981) *Focusing*. Second edition. New York: Bantam Books.

Gendlin, E.T. (1997) *Experiencing and the Creation of Meaning: A Philosophical and Psychological Approach to the Subjective*. Evanston: Northwestern University Press.

Gendlin, E.T. (1997). *Experiencing and the Creation of Meaning: A Philosophical and Psychological Approach to the Subjective*. Evanston: Northwestern University Press.

Gergen, K. (2001). *Social Construction in Context*. London: Sage.

Germer, C., Siegel, R., and Fulton, P. (eds.). (2005). *Mindfulness and Psychotherapy*. New York: The Guilford Press.

Goffman, E. (1959). *The Presentation of Self in Everyday Life*. Harmondsworth: Penguin.

Gomez, L. and Smart, D. (2008). 'Play in practice in psychotherapy and Education'. *European Journal of Psychotherapy, Counselling and Health*, 10:2 147–158.

Hall, C. (1994). *Getting Down to Writing: a students' guide to overcoming writer's block*. Norfolk UK: Peter Francis Publishers.

Hall, C. (2007). Spinning the Threads: the art of conversation, *Therapy Today*, 18 (1).

Harre, R. (ed). (1986). *The Social Construction of Emotions*. Oxford: Basil Blackwell.

Hartmann, E. (1996). 'Outline for a theory on the nature and functions of dreaming'. *Dreaming*, 6:2.

Hermann, J. L. (1992). *Trauma and Recovery*. New York: Basic Books.

Hill, C. (2004). *Dream work in Therapy: Facilitating Exploration, Insight and Action*. Washington DC: American Psychological Assoc. Press.

Hobson, R.F. (1985). *Forms of Feeling: the heart of psychotherapy*. London: Tavistock Publications.

Holm-Brantbjerg, M. (2007). *Muscular Intelligence – an Introduction*, http://www.moaiku.com (accessed on 10/01/2010).

Holmes, J. (1999). 'Narrative, attachment and the therapeutic process' in Mace, C. (ed) *Heart and Soul: The therapeutic face of philosophy*. London: Routledge.

Holmes, J. (2001). *The Secure Base: Attachment theory and psychotherapy*. Hove, East Sussex: Brunner- Routledge, Chapters 7, 8.

Jenkins, R. (2008). *Social Identity*. Third edition. London and New York: Routledge.

Juhan, D. (1987). *Job's Body: A Handbook for Bodywork*. New York: Station Hill Press.

Jung, C. (1933). *Modern Man in search of a soul*. New York: Harvest.

Kearney, A. (1996). *Counselling, Class and Politics*. Ross on Wye: PCCS Books.

Kearney, R. (2004). *On Paul Ricoeur: The Owl of Minerva*. Aldershot: Ashgate.

Keleman, S. (1989). *Your body speaks its mind*. Berkeley, CA: Center Press.

Kernberg, O. (1976). *Object Relations Theory and Clinical Psychoanalysis*. New York: J. Aronson.

Kernberg, O. (1980). *Internal World and External Reality*. New York: J. Aronson.

Kirschenbaum, H. and Henderson, V.L. (eds.). (1990). *Carl Rogers: Dialogues*. London: Constable.

Klein. M. (1957). *Envy, Gratitude and other works: 1946–63*. New York: Delacorte, 1975.

Knowles M. and Moon, R. (2006). *Introducing metaphor*. Oxon UK: Routledge.

Kohut, H. (1977). *The Restoration of the Self*. New York: International Universities Press.

Krause I. (1998). *Therapy Across Culture*. London: Sage.

Lago, C. (2006). *Race, Culture and Counselling: The Ongoing Challenge*. 2nd edition. Milton Keynes: OU Press.

Lago, C. and Smith, B. Eds. (2010). *Anti-Discriminatory Practice in Counselling and Psychotherapy*. 2nd edition, London: Sage.

Leary, M. (2004). *The Curse of the Self*. New York: Oxford University Press.

Levinas, E. (1969). *Totality and infinity: An essay on exteriority*. (Trans. A. Lingis). Pittsburgh: Duquesne University Press.

Levinas, E. (1998). *Otherwise than being: Or beyond essence* (Trans. A. Lingis).

Levithin, D. (2006). *This is Your Brain on Music*. London: Atlantic Books.

Luepnitz, D. (2003). *Schopenhauer's Porcupines: intimacy and its dilemmas*. NY: Basic Books.

Mace, C. (2007). 'Mindfulness in Psychotherapy: An Introduction'. *Advances in Psychiatric Treatment (2007), vol. 13, 147–154*.

Macfarlane, R. (2003). *Mountains of the Mind*. London: Granta Books.

Macfarlane, R. (2007). *The Wild Places*. London: Granta Books.

Maguire, M. (2004). *Men, Women Passion and Power: Gender Issues in Psychotherapy*. Hove: Routledge.

McLeod, J. (1997). *Narrative and Psychotherapy*. London: Sage.

Mead, G.H. (1934). *Mind, Self and Society, from the standpoint of a Social Behaviorist*. Chicago: University of Chicago Press.

Mearns, D. and Thorne B. (2007). *Person-Centred Counselling in Action*.(Third edition.) London: Sage.

Mearns, D. and Thorne, B. (2000). *Person-Centred Therapy Today*. London: Sage.

Meissner, W. (2009). 'Towards a Neurological Reconstruction of Projective. *Journal of the American Psychoanalytic Association, 57*: 95–129.

Menuhin, Y. (1976). *Unfinished Journey*. London: Futura Publications Ltd.

Milner, M. (1990). *On Not Being Able to Paint*. Second ed. Madison: International Universities Press.

Mitchell, S. (1988). *Relational Concepts in Psychoanalysis: An Integration*. Cambridge, Mass: Harvard University Press.

Mitchell, S. (1993). *Hope and Dread in Psychoanalysis*. New York: Basic Books.

Mitchell, S. and Black, M. (1995). *Freud and Beyond*. New York: Basic Books.

Molino A. (ed.) (1996). *Elaborate Selves: Reflections and Reveries of Christopher Bollas, Michael Eigen, Polly Young-Eisendrath, Samuel and Evelyn Laeuchli and Marie Coleman Nelson*. Worcester UK; Clunie Press.

Moon, L. (ed). (2008). *Feeling Queer or Queer Feelings? Radical Approaches to Counselling Sex, Sexualities and Genders*. London and New York: Routledge.

Moore, J. and C. Purton (eds.). (2006). *Spirituality and Counselling: Experiential and Theoretical Perspectives.* Ross-on-Wye: PCCS Books.

Morrison, B. (2008). The Reading Cure. *The Guardian*, 05.01.08.

Muldoon, M. (2002). *On Ricoeur.* Belmont, CA: Wadsworth.

O'Keeffe, G. (1926). From the Foreword to the Catalogue of her Show at the Anderson Galleries in New York, 1926.

Oatley, K. (2008). The Mind's Flight Simulator. *The Psychologist*, 21:1030–1032.

Pargament, K.I. (2007). *Spiritually Integrated Psychotherapy: Understanding and Addressing the Sacred.* New York: The Guilford Press.

Proctor, G. (2002). *Dynamics of Power in Counselling and Psychotherapy: Ethics, Politics and Practice.* Ross-on-Wye: PCCS Books.

Reay. D. (2005). 'Beyond Consciousness? The Psychic Landscape of Social Class'. *Sociology,* 39,5 911–928.

Reik, T. (1948). *Listening with the Third Ear: The inner experience of a psychoanalyst.* New York: Grove Press.

Ricoeur, P. (1975). *The Rule of Metaphor.* London: Routledge & Kegan Paul.

Ricoeur, P. (1978). *The Rule of Metaphor: Multi-disciplinary Studies of the Creation of Meaning in Language.* (Translators: Robert Czerny, Kathleen McLaughlin and John Costello, SJ.) London: Routledge.

Ricoeur, P. (1998). *Oneself as Another.* (Translator: Kathleen Blamey.) Chicago: University of Chicago Press.

Rogers, C. (1951). *Client-Centered Therapy.* London: Constable.

Rogers, C. (1963). The Actualizing Tendency in Relation to "Motives" and to Consciousness. In M.R. Jones (ed.) *Nebraska Symposium on Motivation.* Lincoln: University of Nebraska Press, 1–24.

Rogers, C. (1967). *On becoming a person: A therapist's view of psychotherapy.* London: Constable.

Rogers, C.R. (1951). *Client-Centered Therapy.* London, Constable.

Rose, C. (2007). 'The Internal and External Group'. *Therapy Today*, 18, 5.

Rose, C. (2008). *The Personal Development Group: The Students' Guide.* London: Karnac.

Roszak, T. (1996). *Ecopsychology.* San Francisco: Sierra Club Books.

Rowan, J. (1990). *Subpersonalities: The People Inside Us.* London: Routledge.

Rust, M-J. (2008). *Consuming the Earth: Unconscious Processes in Relation to Our Environmental Crisis.* Keynote Lecture for Climate of Change conference, Bristol. 2008. http://www.mjrust.net/downloads/Consuming the Earth.pdf (accessed 9.07.2010)

Sartre, J-P. (1969). *Being and Nothingness.* London: Routledge.

Schaverien, J. (1992). *The Revealing Image: Analytical Art Psychotherapy in Theory and Practice.* London: Routledge.

Seigel, J. (2005). *The Idea of the Self: Thought and Experience in Western Europe Since the Seventeenth Century.* Cambridge: Cambridge University Press.

Stacey, R. (2003) *Complexity and Group Processes: A Radically Social Understanding of Individuals.* Hove: Routledge.

Stamm, B. H. (1995). *Secondary Traumatic Stress: Self-care issues for Clinicians, Researchers, and Educators.* Baltimore: Sidran Press.

Stern, D. N. (1985). *The interpersonal world of the infant. A view from psychoanalysis and developmental psychology.* New York: Basic Books.

Stern, D. N. (2004). *The Present Moment: In Psychotherapy and Everyday Life*. New York: Norton.

Taylor, C. (1989). *Sources of the Self: The Making of Modern Identity*. Cambridge: Cambridge University Press.

Trevarthen, C. (1979). 'Communication and cooperation in early infancy: A description of primary intersubjectivity'. In M Bullova, ed., *Before speech: The beginning of human communication*, pp. 321–347. Cambridge: Cambridge University Press.

Ullman, M. (1996). *Appreciating Dreams- a group approach*. Thousand Oaks, CA: Sage.

Wachtel, P. (2008). *Relational Theory and the Practice of Psychotherapy*. New York; Guilford.

Walkerdine, V., Lucey, H., and Melody, J. (2002). *Growing Up Girl: Psychosocial explorations of Gender & Class*. London: Palgrave.

Waller, D., and Gilroy, A. (eds.). (1992). *Art Therapy: A Handbook*. Buckingham: Open University Press.

Wetherell, M. (ed.). (2009). *Identity in the 21st Century: New Trends in Changing Times*. Basingstoke: Palgrave.

Wetherell, M. and Talpade Mohanty, C. (eds.). (2010). *The Sage Handbook of Identities*. London: Sage.

Wheeler, S. and Richards, K. (2007). 'The impact of clinical supervision on counsellors and therapists, their practice and their clients. A systematic review of the literature'. *Counselling and Psychotherapy Research* 7 (1): 54–65.

William, R. (2009). 'Using dreams to train the reflective practitioner: the Ullman dream group in social work education', *Reflective Practice*, 10: 5, 577 – 587.

Wilson, S. (2003). *Disability, Counselling and Psychotherapy*. Hampshire and New York: Palgrave Macmillan.

Winnicott, D. (1953). Transitional objects and transitional phenomena. *International Journal of Psychoanalysis*, 34:89–97.

Winnicott, D. (1965). *The Maturational Process and the Facilitating Environment*. London: Hogarth. Reprinted 2007, London: Karnac.

Winnicott, D. W. (1971). *Playing and Reality*. Harmondsworth: Penguin Books.

Winnicott, D. W. (1971). *Playing and Reality*. Harmondsworth: Penguin Books.

Winterson, J. (2008). Shafts of Sunlight. *The Guardian*, 15.11.08.

Woodward, K. (ed.). (2004). *Questioning Identity: Gender, Class, Ethnicity*. 2nd edition. London and New York: Routledge.

Worsley, R. (2006). Emmanuel Levinas: Resource and challenge for therapy. *PCEP* 5:3, 208–20.

Worsley, R. (2009). *Process Work in Person-Centred Therapy: Phenomenological and Existential Perspectives*. (Second edition). London: Palgrave.

Wright, J. K. (2009). Dialogical journal writing as 'self-therapy': 'I matter', *Counselling and Psychotherapy Research*, 9(4): 234–40.

Yalom, I. (2005). *The Schopenhauer Cure: A Novel*. New York: Harper Collins.

Youell, B. (2008). 'The importance of play and playfulness.' *European Journal of Psychotherapy and Counselling*, 10:2 121–129.

Index